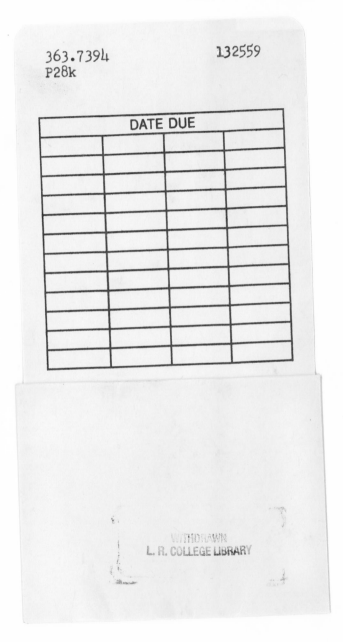

A Killing Rain

A Killing Rain

The Global Threat of Acid Precipitation

Thomas Pawlick

Sierra Club Books • San Francisco

Library of Congress Cataloging in Publication Data

Pawlick, Thomas.
    A killing rain.

    Includes index.
    1. Acid deposition—Canada. 2. Acid deposition—United States. I. Title.
TD19.6.A25P38   1984   363.7'394   84–5367
ISBN 0–87156–823–3

Jacket design Copyright © 1984 by Lawrence Ratzkin
Book design by Nancy Warner
Printed in the United States of America
10 9 8 7 6 5 4 3 2

for Peg, Ruth and Ed

Contents

Preface

"Sexy" issues are as changeable in politics as rock bands are in pop music. They rise, peak and eventually fall from public attention with sometimes astonishing speed. In a presidential election year the rising and falling occur at an even faster rate, as campaign managers experiment first with one, then another symbol for their candidates to brandish. Like the contestants themselves, issues that lack staying power tend to fade in the primaries. Only the truly tough ones survive.

In this context, it will be interesting to see what happens to the issue of acid deposition—better known by the less accurate title of acid rain. As a physical phenomenon, acid rain has been around a long time. The term itself was coined in England in the early 1900's by scientists studying the effects of coal burning on local crops. As a major political issue in countries other than the United States it has also been around for awhile—more than ten years in Europe and at least five in Canada.

At this writing, however, acid rain is just beginning to hit the charts in the U.S., hovering down around eight or nine among the top ten subjects of controversy. Where will it be by November? Perhaps the politicians will have had a great game with it, kicking the new football around, scoring points against opponents, racking up numbers in the polls. Perhaps it may not have proven sexy enough, ending its election year career in limbo.

While the posturing goes on, however, the rain will keep falling, and unlike the promises of politicians its effects are real. The damage being done is factual, physical and in too many cases irreparable. Time is running out. Even if Congress should temporarily save the day and come through with a compromise abatement bill before the 1984 election, a tremendous amount of damage will still be done before controls can actually be put in place.

Given the strength of any such bill's opponents—chief among them the Reagan administration—it is entirely possible that its restrictions may not be strong enough or that, under an executive branch firmly opposed to pollution control, enforcement of the law could be lax.

The situation is fluid, chancey. The prospects are uncertain.

It would be pleasant to discover, at some future date, that this book played even a small part in tipping the scales in favor of the environment—and that they tipped when it still counted, before it was too late.

T. Pawlick
February 1984

A Killing Rain

One

The Acid Earth

I t begins with heat: jets of coal dust and air bursting into flame at 3,500° F in the fire chambers of electric power plants; molten sulphide ores bubbling and blistering in smelter furnaces; gasoline exploding at 4,500° F under the steel cylinder heads of trucks, buses and automobiles; diesel oil, Exxon regular, bituminous coal, anthracite, lignite, the ores of nickel and copper, pyrrhotite, pentlandite, niccolite, chrysolite, burning until the heat cracks their internal electron bonds and breaks each compound into its constituents, to rise, as gases, vapor or microscopic particles, into the air.

"Precursors," chemists call them, harbingers of things to come.

Because of them, and their end products, 50,000 to 200,000 people with asthma or other lung disorders will die prematurely this year. Because of them, relations between the United States and Canada have fallen to their lowest point in decades. Because of them, whole sectors of such industries as lumber, paper and pulp, inland sport and commercial fishing, tourism and agriculture could face losses ranging from millions of dollars per year to bankruptcy. The maple sugar industry in Vermont and Quebec is threatened. The sport fishery in Ontario, Nova Scotia and upstate New York has sustained heavy losses. Corrosion damage to homes, buildings, outdoor monuments and vehicles across the continent exceeds $2 billion per year.

Because of the heat and the smoke, something has come into existence that wasn't here before.

At American Electric Power Company's General James M. Gavin plant, a 2.6-million-kilowatt generating complex whose thousand-foot, dun-colored smokestack juts up from the banks of the Ohio River near the town of Cheshire, Ohio, the fuel for the fire comes in great batches—600 tons of coal an hour for each of the installation's boilers. So much coal is needed to run the 25-story units that AEP, whose multistate power grid has ranked for years among the nation's worst polluters, has to operate its own mines, three of them, just to supply Gavin. Millions of tons of coal flow each year along a 10-mile-long conveyor belt that winds across the wooded hills of rural Meigs County from the mines to the plant. But even this mountain of black rock, ripped from the earth by the revolving steel teeth of "continuous mining" machines run by an army of 1,800 miners and their support staff, isn't enough. Still more coal must be brought in from other sources, by railroad car and river barges, to feed the flames that change water into steam and turn the huge station's turbines.

Men in hard hats, gray twill jumpsuits and black rubber boots, engineers, technicians, laborers and miners, do the heavy work, taking and giving orders in the twangy, half-Southern drawl of the Ohio/Kentucky border region. They work in heat and dirt and constant noise, in the mines where digging and air-circulation equipment roar, in the coal preparation plant where clattering machines crush and crack the coal, press it, bathe it in water and filter it, in the power plant itself, where fire and steam and the wild whine of the turbines drown even the loudest shout.

The washing process they oversee in the preparation plant removes impurities from the coal that could cut the efficiency of Gavin's boilers. Along with ash, a certain amount of sulphur-containing compounds, called pyrites, are taken away by rinsing the coal and passing it through various meshes until the heavier pyrite settles out. But not all of the 3.7 percent sulphur in the fuel mined for Gavin comes in pyrite form. In fact, only 0.2 percent is eliminated by washing. The rest, with nitrogen, hydrogen, oxygen and a long list of trace metals and other elements chemically bonded to the carbon in the coal, is separable only by burning.

When the coal does burn, as hard-hatted technicians watch the dials, buttons, gauges and warning lights that make the plant's control room look like the bridge of a space ship, its sulphur is released as SO_2—poisonous sulphur dioxide gas— and its nitrogen as toxic nitrogen oxides (NO_x). Equally toxic trace elements, chiefly mercury, arsenic and aluminum but including nearly 50 others, volatilize or escape as minute particles, and the Gavin smokestack, at 1,103 feet among the highest in the United States, carries them aloft, into the atmosphere, into the infinite chemical complexity of the air, to react and be reacted upon.

Hundreds of power plants across the United States and Canada follow similar cycles 24 hours a day, around the clock, with more than 60 of the largest, their power outputs greater than 50 megawatts each, clustered in the Ohio Valley alone. Together, the makers of electricity contribute more than half of the 35 million tons of SO_2 released each year from man-made sources in North America, and a quarter of the 24.5 million tons of NO_x. The rest comes mainly from ore smelters, other industrial boilers, home heating and from the exhaust pipes of cars, trucks and other vehicles, which exhale only a tiny fraction of SO_2 but emit more than 40 percent of the total NO_x.

The smoke flies up.

Compressed and placed on the balance tray of a vast, imaginary scale, the daily continental emissions of sulphur and nitrogen oxides would weigh more than 163,013 tons: the equivalent, by weight, of 4,075 fully loaded railroad freight cars being tossed into the air every day.

And they mark only the starting point. Though toxic in themselves, their function is preliminary.

The tall stacks that bear so much of this initial burden were mainly built between the late 1950s and the early 70s, when fear for the environment was growing into a major political issue and the original Clean Air Acts were being passed in the United States and Canada. The stacks marked a crucial departure then, an engineering milestone that seemed to bring genuine blessings in the control of local air pollution.

Nowhere were such blessings more needed than in the northern Canadian mining town of Sudbury, Ontario, a city whose name has become symbolic of the ills of industrialism.

Wounded Sudbury. Like the victim of some terrible, violent crime, it stirs first pity, then outrage, then admiration. Its people refuse to give up, despite a century of corporate pillage. They hang on. They would make rocks bloom.

Their community was once a forest and subsequently, after 19th-century lumberjacks clear-cut many of the trees to supply railroad ties for the Canadian Pacific Railway, a region of thriving farms. Then came doom. In 1883 rich deposits of nickel and copper that had been ignored for 30 years were rediscovered, and by 1886 a group of American investors, forerunners of today's Inco Limited (until 1976 called the International Nickel Company) had begun mining and smelting operations in the area.

The first crude smelter, located five miles outside of Sudbury at Copper Cliff, employed a method called "heap roasting." Raw ore was simply dumped on top of great piles of cordwood, cut from what was left of the already depleted forests, then set ablaze and allowed to smolder for months, until the metal separated from the rock. Thick blankets of foul, sulphurous fumes smothered the surrounding region, choking, deadly. Later smelting methods employed by various mining companies attracted to the area, though slightly less crude, did little to thin the clouds of sulphur oxides, or the shower of copper, nickel, zinc and other toxic metal particles that accompanied them.

Gradually, over the years, almost everything that had been alive in the smelters' vicinity—except the ruthlessly exploited mine and smelter workers and their families—died. Farmers went bankrupt, their crops withered. The last remnants of the original white pine forest faded away. The paint on the workers' houses peeled. The miners themselves, their lungs ravaged with every breath drawn above or below ground, inside the smelters or out, endured bronchitis, silicosis, lung fibrosis, cancer and skin diseases, while their city became a national joke: The booby prize in a Canadian raffle was an all-expenses-paid trip to Sudbury.

The price of this corporate vandalism in damage to human health, vegetation and property was set in a 1974 federal government report (*The Sudbury Pollution Problem: Socio-Economic Background*, Environment Canada, unpublished) at $465,850,000 per year.

By 1970, however, the national mood had begun to change. Like its American counterpart, Canadian public opinion had responded to the environmental movement of the 60s by bringing heavy pressure to bear on the politicians who had given companies like Inco free rein for decades. The company, whose Copper Cliff smelter had been pouring out 6,000 tons of SO$_2$ *per day* throughout the previous years, making it the largest single source of sulphur pollution in North America, was at last ordered by a reluctant Ontario government to begin cleaning up. The order called for a moderate initial drop in daily emissions to 5,200 tons, followed by a reduction to 3,600 tons by 1976. It also mandated replacement of the smelter's three 500-foot-and-under chimneys with a much taller new stack "to dilute and thus disperse the smelter's gases" away from the city of Sudbury.

Actually, as an Inco vice-president noted in a published report, the company had decided on its own, three years earlier, to build such a stack as the most economical way to comply with the local ambient air standards of the government of Ontario Air Pollution Act, 1967. The chimney it had already decided to erect would come eventually to be known as the Superstack—1,250 feet tall, the highest chimney in the world.

The best way to see it is alone, on foot, from across the miles of barrens that surround the stack's approach—a landscape from a nightmare, more sinister than Tolkien's Land of Mordor "where the shadows lie," because its shadows are real.

Charred black rock, its granite face pitted with tiny holes like the surface of a sponge, seems to stretch forever in all directions, jagged and bare. No trees grow, no grass, not even weeds. There are no birds. No insects buzz. The sound of a rock dislodged by a climber's foot echoes in emptiness as it clatters down the bleak slopes. Here and there, in the hollows between hills, the smashed gray branches and trunk of a long-dead pine are strewn in a heap, like bleached driftwood. A steady wind scours the rubble, whipping at pant legs. Nearer to the plant the sound of seagulls can be heard, and a solitary black crow sails overhead: There is a garbage dump near the smelter, an island of filthy but nevertheless organic detritus for scavengers to feed upon.

And then there is the stack. It looms over the crest of a hill, distant, wrapped in haze, flanked by the smaller chimneys it replaced. White aircraft warning lights near its top flash intermittently, tiny specks far away, and the stack plume, a miles-long trail of gas, streams like a great white banner against the sky, east and south. Its silence is striking. It seems alive.

Because of the stack's height, the acrid sulphurous fumes that once strangled Sudbury no longer touch ground near the smelter itself. Often as hot as 700° F, rushing up the stack at 55 miles per hour, they debouch instead into a higher air layer. Sudbury's air, in consequence, is measurably cleaner. The city can breathe at last, and in that limited sense the Superstack has fulfilled a purpose. But company claims in 1970 that the stack would prove "the quickest remedy for sulphur dioxide" have proven to be a myth, as have similar claims by the American factories and utilities that also chose tall stacks as a panacea. (In the Ohio Valley, the average stack height of electric power generating stations in 1950 was 320 feet. By 1980 it had risen to 740 feet, with numerous stacks towering over the 1,000-foot mark.)

The tall stacks carried gases up and away from the local communities, but they did not eliminate the problem. The fumes were simply blown further afield, to other communities downwind. Worse: In traveling the gases had time to metamorphose, reacting with the rich variety of chemicals in the atmosphere and taking on new forms—more dangerous forms. In dispersing the fumes, the tall stacks are spreading a plague.

Studies conducted for the U.S. Environmental Protection Agency (EPA) and other scientific bodies have begun to reveal the complicated mechanisms involved, starting with the fate of the initial stream of hot gases as they emerge from a smokestack. *Erupt* may be a better word. Moving at 50 miles an hour or better, they can shoot in seconds to levels double the stack's actual height—to more than 2,200 feet in the case of the Gavin plant. Then, bending horizontally under the pressure of the prevailing wind, the gases stream away in a widening plume.

In simplified terms, what happens next depends on several variables, including the season of the year, local weather conditions and the contour of the surrounding land surfaces. On a warm summer morning in the Ohio Valley, a moving plume emitted at 7 A.M. might retain a fairly compact shape, traveling east and north with prevailing air currents for up to 20 miles. Then around midmorning, as the air near ground level warms in response to the heating of the soil by the sun, an unstable "mixing layer" of shifting air currents develops and grows. This layer, rising gradually from the land surface toward the plume overhead, finally contacts and captures the plume, dispersing its gases in every direction from 4,500 feet to ground level. By 6 P.M., diffused particles from the original plume may have touched ground up to 100 miles away from the stack that emitted them that morning.

At night or in winter a plume can travel even farther in the same amount of time. After sundown the mixing layer collapses, leaving the upper air vertically stable. A plume emitted at night may thus remain "decoupled" from the ground, be picked up by a nocturnal jet stream—a high-altitude river of air coursing through the atmosphere at velocities of 130 miles an hour or higher—and be blown 200 miles downwind before the next day's mixing layer even begins to develop.

In winter, cooler temperatures also prevent daytime mixing layers from rising to much more than half their normal summer altitudes. Only rarely do they reach as high as the crest of a tall stack. As a result, winter stack plumes can stay decoupled from the surface for not hours but days, traveling 300 or 400 miles, sometimes more, before starting to break up.

They do not, of course, travel alone. Other plumes from other stacks move with, around and through them, as do particles from the so-called "urban plumes" that envelop major cities in a pall of auto exhaust, heating and factory smoke. These amorphous metropolitan clouds, more diffuse than tall stack plumes because they emerge near the surface and well within the mixing layer, are made up chiefly of nitrogen oxides and hydrocarbons. Their well-stirred contents can nonetheless waft as high as the passing tall stack gases, meet and blend with them and, eventually, filter with them back to earth.

The journey down is often a slow process, and what finally touches ground may be entirely different from what the stacks and auto tailpipes sent up. A recent attempt to outline what happens chemically when SO_2 reacts with only *one* atmospheric component—the hydroxyl radical, HO—ran to no fewer than 17 lines of chemical equations. Whole pages of formulae have been elaborated to try to describe the interactions between sulphur and nitrogen oxides and the ozone, water vapor, carbon dioxide, methane, hydrocarbon pollutants and a host of other substances in the air. The authors of an EPA report summarizing the state of current scientific knowledge of the subject were forced to admit "we are still struggling to assemble . . . the individual pieces."

Two things nevertheless are certain: Whatever the intermediate steps in sulphur dioxide's interactions, eventually it combines with the moisture in the atmosphere to become H_2SO_4—sulphuric acid—while the oxides of nitrogen end their aerial wanderings as HNO_3, nitric acid. Floating and falling, rising and shifting among clouds and currents of air, they exist as aerosols, finer than the spray of the sea, suspended, waiting. Acids in an acid sky.

Sulphuric acid, also known as oil of vitriol, is one of the most corrosive chemicals known. Oily and colorless, it can char living tissue on contact. Nitric acid, known to medieval alchemists as *aqua fortis*—strong water—is equally caustic, capable of causing severe burns.

Of course, diluted in the atmosphere neither acid is strong enough to produce burns on contact. A skydiver falling through the clouds would not notice their presence, would feel no sting on his skin as he passed. But they are there, invisible and insidious. And slowly, in increments so small at first as to have been almost imperceptible, they have had effect. They have changed, in fact, the very nature of rain and snow.

The acidity of various substances, from soil to seawater, is usually measured on the pH scale. The abbreviation pH, standing for "potential hydrogen," refers to the number of positively charged hydrogen ions (H^+) concentrated in a substance, as opposed to the concentration of negatively charged hydroxyl ions (OH^-). An ion, or electrically charged particle, is formed when the atoms of a chemical element gain or lose one or more of the electrons that spin around in their outer shells. If the atoms lose electrons they become positively charged, and are known as "cations"; if they take on extra electrons they become negatively charged: "anions." Hydrogen cations are formed when acids are dissolved in water and break up, or dissociate. Sulphuric acid, for instance, dissociates into hydrogen cations (H^+H^+) and sulphate anions (SO_4^{--}). When bases are dissolved in water they form hydroxides.

On the pH scale, which runs from 0 to 14, the number seven is neutral. Anything above seven is basic; anything below it is acidic. For example, pure distilled water has a pH of seven, while vinegar has a pH of 2.5 and an alkaline substance such as baking soda has a pH of 8.5. Because the pH scale is logarithmic, each change of one unit represents a change in ion concentration 10 times that of the number nearest it. Thus pH 4 is 10 times more acidic than pH 5, and pH 3 is 100 times more.

Ordinarily, unpolluted rainfall in most temperate regions is usually mildly acidic—around pH 5.6—due to the presence in the air of small amounts of naturally formed carbonic and acetic acids. Both are relatively weak compounds whose effects are easily offset, or buffered, by the normal alkalinity of lakes and soils. Sulphuric and nitric acids, in contrast, are strong inorganic compounds whose presence can drastically lower pH and whose effects are not easily neutralized. Only an area with a relatively thick organic humus layer, or one formed from limestone or other calcareous bedrocks, has sufficient reserves of alkalinity to counterbalance these two inorganic compounds for more than a few years. Dissolved in rain and snow, they constitute both a quantitatively greater and qualitatively new force.

Historical weather records in both Europe and North America are scattered and sometimes inconsistent, but the evidence that is available shows an undeniable and an increasingly rapid change in the acidity of precipitation in the northern hemisphere. Samples taken in Greenland of glacial ice formed from snow that fell 180 years ago, before the Industrial Revolution, show pH levels ranging from 6 to 7.6. The earliest known measurement of precipitation pH in the United States, taken in Maine in 1939 by Henry G. Houghton of the Massachusetts Institute of Technology, was 5.9. From 1959 to 1966 the U.S. Public Health Service and National Center for Atmospheric Research took monthly samples of rain and snow at 30 stations around the country, and during the latter part of the period pH readings below 5.6 showed up frequently east of the Mississippi. In the New York/New England region readings of 4.4 were common by 1966. By 1979, the annual average mean pH of precipitation in parts of New York State, Pennsylvania and Ontario was 4.1; in New England, 4.4.

Not only are pH levels apparently falling, but the area affected by the phenomenon seems to be spreading. Thirty years ago, only the Northeastern states were affected, with annual precipitation pH averages of 4.5 to 5. Other states, in the South and East, showed averages of 5 to 5.6 or above. By

1975–76, however, the average annual pH as far south as the Carolinas and as far west as the Mississippi had dropped to 4.5. Only in the southern half of Florida was the average pH above 5. According to a recent report of the Clean Air Coalition, rainfall in the Northeastern United States now averages pH 4 to 4.3.

Individual rain and snow storms, and annual spring thaws that can release a winter's accumulation of snow in a week, produce sudden, short-term "pulses" of strong acidity far in excess of yearly averages. A single summer thunderstorm, for example, may generate precipitation a hundred times as acidic as the seasonal average. One storm in Wheeling, West Virginia, produced rain at an incredible pH 1.5—the equivalent in corrosive strength to the acid in an automobile battery.

Gradually, at a rate of several hundred miles every few years, a blanket of acidified air, laced with intermittent acid pulses of lethal potency, is spreading like an amoeba west and south across the country.

Rain, snow, fog—every form of moisture that falls from the sky east of the Mississippi—has now become acid: acid mist, acid smog, acid sleet, acid hail. Even the dust that flies is acid. Its sulphur-laden particles, described by scientists as "dry deposition" when they fall, contribute a substantial share to the overall burden of acidity building up on the land.

Nor is the phenomenon limited only to the East, or to North America. A less drastic but nevertheless measurable change has also been noted in several Western states, particularly freeway-paved, smog-plagued California, while the air over Europe, stoked by the factories, power plants and automobiles of England, Germany, Russia, Poland, Czechoslovakia and other industrial countries, is if anything more degraded than that over the United States and Canada. The entire northern hemisphere is affected.

Showering farmland and forest canopy, flowing down tree

trunks and plant stems to the ground, acidified rain injures leaf surfaces, upsets the chemical balance of the soil and leaches vital nutrients away from roots. Percolating through layers of humus, it destroys needed soil bacteria and releases toxic metals normally held inert in mineral compounds. Trees and sensitive crops, especially those on land whose acidity has not been offset by liming, die.

Falling on the surface of the water, swelling tributaries during spring runoff, acid rain and melting snow turn ponds and lakes into chemical sinks, killing plankton, insects, frogs and fish. Coating the surfaces of statues, building stone and the steel skins of cars and trucks, the acids corrode and rust and eat them away.

Inhaled as aerosols, the acids attack human lungs, choke asthmatic children, cut off the breathing of the elderly and the ill. The metals they mobilize from the soil, especially mercury and aluminum, poison wells and reservoirs, load the flesh of the fish anglers eat, join with dissolved copper and lead from plumbing pipes and taint the water supply. Kidney patients whose dialysis machines have inadvertently used water sources contaminated with aluminum have already felt the effects, some of them fatal.

The people of Eastern Canada, which receives three to four times more sulphur pollution from the United States than it exports south, and New York and New England, the hardest hit parts of the United States, are in a virtual state of environmental emergency. And it is only a matter of time before they are joined by others.

Flowing with the shift and flux of atmospheric currents that are the breathing of the planet, the legacy of Sudbury, the message etched in the pitted black rocks of the ruined world of Copper Cliff and the ruined lungs of its miners, is moving around the globe.

What once were cleansing rains now wash an acid earth.

Two

Flowers at a Funeral

H er manner is gruff, no-nonsense. Her voice is strong and decisive. She seems the sort of person who *would* fight City Hall, or a parking ticket, or a feuding neighbor—and win. In the Victorian Age, people might have called her "an independent woman." But there is a tinge of regret in her tone; a note of sadness, of a chapter being closed.

Mrs. Donald Strath is 52 years old and getting ready to say goodbye to a large part of her life, to more than three decades' worth of memories. She is selling her home on Dickie Lake, near Baysville, Ontario, in the heart of Canada's famed Muskoka/Haliburton cottage country.

"I've lost interest in the lake," she says. "It's not the same anymore."

The Muskoka region, 100 miles north of Toronto on Highway 11, includes some of the most picturesque natural scenery in the province: deep gorges, rolling spruce- and hardwood-forested hills, spectacular outcrops of rock and hundreds of lakes, ponds and streams. To the east of it along Highway 60 is the wooded fastness of Algonquin Park, a 5,000-square-mile wilderness unmarred by roads, where moose, black bear and deer roam freely and the only form of travel is by canoe or foot. To the west, 35 miles as the crow flies, is the open water of Georgian Bay, a yachtsman's paradise and vacation ground of the rich for more than a century.

Muskoka lies between these extremes, geographically and socially. If Algonquin is the refuge of the rugged and Georgian Bay the playground of the pampered, Muskoka is a place of middle-class dreams, a weekend retreat for Toronto families of more or less ordinary income, whose savings must be patiently budgeted to pay for a cottage and boat, fishing rods, water skis and a card table for Saturday-night euchre. There are wealthy cottagers here, but they are a minority among a summer population of teachers, small-business owners and civil servants and the year-round core of area natives—part-time farmers or auto mechanics who operate campgrounds and marinas in season and make a major part of their living from the tourist trade.

The middle class, the social bedrock on which Canada is built, finds its escape and recreation on these lakes, and now the quality of its hard-earned haven is in danger.

"I was born here in this area," says Mrs. Strath. "I've owned this land since the end of the Second World War. I bought it off my Dad and I held it a long time, until Don and I got married 30 years ago and we built a cottage. We had our home in King City, but my husband is disabled and when he quit working we sold that and moved back here. We built a permanent home near the cottage.

"It used to be beautiful sandy beach here. I have pictures of the beach originally and its clean, white sand. But for the last five or six years it's gotten bad. We get all this dirty, slimy, greenish muck in our bay, a thick slime that turns into brown sludge around the mouth of the creek that feeds the lake. It's all through the water, just floating. The whole bay was practically taken over. Neilsons next door complained about it and it's all over the lake, in different people's bays. I worried about it because of people swimming in it, and I wrote to the Ministry of Natural Resources about it."

The ministry sent a technician down to take samples, and, several weeks later, Mrs. Strath received a letter. "Thank you for contacting the ministry," it said, and explained that the slime consisted of various species of filamentous algae, mostly of the species "*Mougeotia* . . . which appears to be indicative of increasing acidity of lake water." The ministry added, by way of reassurance, that "none of these filamentous algae pose a health hazard."

"I wouldn't go in it," says Mrs. Strath. "I wouldn't swim in it, hazardous or not."

The couple—she a former office worker, retired from the teletype section of CPR Communications (Canada's equivalent of Western Union), he a former municipal stockbroker forced by a heart attack to stop working—are in many ways typical of the area. But Mrs. Strath has also earned a measure of local fame. She is a skillful fisherwoman whose record-size catches have placed her among the region's outdoor elite. Although she downplays her achievements, it is obvious, listening to her, that fishing has been one of the great joys of her life.

"Years ago this [Dickie Lake] used to be a good bass lake, smallmouth bass. There were perch, bullheads and sunfish and even, years ago, the odd trout. But the fishing's very poor now," she says. "I used to fish quite a bit, but I haven't even wet a line this summer. I figure it's not worth my while.

"I've had the trophy several years, with four-pounders. My name's on the Dickie Lake trophy three times. I used live bait. I had a rod with a flyline on it and I just reeled out a bunch of line, put it in the bottom of my boat and when the bass took it I let him run with it. And then I snagged 'em. I had three goes at the trophy and then I kind of let up. I figured it was up to some of the other people to get it once in awhile. Kids like to get it, so why should I? I'm here year-round when they're not and can fish from first of bass season to the end of November.

"But now nobody's getting any big fish. The fishing's gone. There was a meeting in the hall last year and apparently they did a survey on this lake and they notified us then that there were no new fish coming on. What fish there were in the lake were medium-size ones and when they grew up or died there would be no new ones to take their place. The small ones aren't there. The people from the ministry who held the meeting said it was the acid rain leaching things from the soil into the water that kills them.

"What's the point, then, in my going out there?"

The fish aren't the only things disappearing from Dickie Lake. Frogs and crayfish, the traditional live-bait standbys for bass fishermen, are also vanishing: "We have very few frogs anymore," says Mrs. Strath. "We used to have an awful lot of pollywogs on our beach, the baby frogs, but we haven't got any anymore. And the lake was good for crayfish. There's none anymore. Can't find any anywhere.

"When we were camping up at Horn Lake you could get all kinds of them up there. I brought a lot of crayfish back and put them in our lake thinking they'd multiply and help the population come back. But they didn't. You can't find any. I think I put over 200 in, but now, no crayfish in the lake.

"They claim that, when a lake goes acid, the frogs and the crayfish are the first to go.

"I don't go fishing anymore. If I did, I think I'd head out to another lake somewhere. This one's a waste of time. The fish just aren't there anymore. We're trying to sell the house and I think if we sold it we'd sell the cottage too because I've lost interest in the lake. I always swore I'd never sell the cottage, but I don't know, now."

No fishing, and green slime to swim in—and these are only indicators of greater changes to come.

In 1983 an unusually dry July apparently had an adverse effect on the blooms of acid-tolerant algae fouling Dickie Lake, and the beaches were temporarily white again throughout most of that August. But the big fish have not come back, nor are they likely to.

There have been other reasons, including an influx of noisy power boaters, that have influenced the Straths' decision to sell. But the decline in the basic quality of the lake evidently has been a leading factor. Like others in the area, they have realized it may be irreversible.

The Muskoka/Haliburton region, much like the salmon rivers of Nova Scotia, the La Cloche lakes of Killarney, Ontario, and bodies of water in the Adirondack area of upstate New York, where similar things have happened, has two strikes against it: First, its shallow soils and rocks in many locations have little natural ability to offset, or buffer, increases in acidity. Second, its geographical position, described by one resident as "ground zero," is such that acid plumes from both the Midwestern United States *and* Sudbury pass over it, borne on the wind.

The pH of some lakes in the territory is still close to neutral, while that of others seems to fluctuate with the "pulses" of individual rainstorms. But the pH of an alarming number of lakes has fallen from highs near 7 down to 6 and even 5.3 during the past decade. An estimated 140 acidified lakes in Ontario have already lost their fish populations, and many lakes in this region may soon lose theirs. The number of empty lakes is expected to rise dramatically over the next ten years. According to a 1981 survey, more than 2,000 Ontario lakes have a pH below 5, while at least 27,000 more are vulnerable to rapid acidification. In 20 years, according to some estimates, more than 40,000 could be affected.

Studies cited by the U.S. Environmental Protection Agency indicate that wide areas of the continent, containing hundreds of thousands of lakes and waterways, are similarly vulnerable.

Eighty percent of New England is considered highly sensitive, as are the Allegheny, Smoky and Rocky mountains, most of Eastern Canada and parts of the coastal Southeast and the Northwestern and North Central United States.

People who live near affected lakes are worried, and angry. Not far from the town of Dorset, a few miles east of Dickie Lake, teacher and part-time fur trapper John McLennan, 49, has watched the changes in his own and other locations. He lives on the shore of Paint Lake.

"Plastic Lake near here used to be called Pine Lake originally and I went in there fishing for rainbow trout," he recalls. "I paddled a canoe for a doctor who was interested in fly fishing, back in the mid-1960s, and the rainbow were jumping all around us. The pH there now [according to a recent government test, 5.6] is too low for trout. Rainbows don't even last 24 hours when introduced to it. They're finished. And they ship them off to labs in Toronto, where they find aluminum collected in the gills.

"This property here [on Paint Lake] I've used for 17 summers as a public campground, and I vividly remember that in 1969 campers started complaining at noon that the beach smelled. It was the bodies of dead bullfrog tadpoles, and they were here in enough number that I had to go down to the beach with a hand rake, raking away the dead tadpoles. I kept that up until 1973 and after that I didn't have to rake any more tadpoles. Bullfrogs used to be a real chorus at night here, but we no longer see them. I heard just one out here this year, and I had one sitting in a brush pile down the creek for part of last summer and he did a bit of croaking. But I've never seen any reproduction since about '73.

"Something else that bothered me was that when we first started here with campers and lots of swimming activity the campers complained about stepping on clamshells. A muskrat was collecting clams and going under the dock, cracking them open and taking the goodies, and leaving the shells there. And about the same time the bullfrog tadpoles stopped washing up on the beach I noticed that we also weren't getting the clams any longer."

A quiet-spoken man with graying hair, McLennan began his story sitting back, relaxed, on the sofa in his living room. But as he continues, he becomes more intense, moving to the edge of his seat and leaning over the coffee table on which the spools of a tape recorder silently turn.

"There is something else too," he says. "We received with our tax bill this summer a notice from the government saying that we should run our water for a period of time before we drink it, because by checking well water throughout the area— my well was checked so it's part of the calculations—they've noticed that the pH in well water is dropping!"

The notice, under the heading "BULLETIN" in huge green letters, is from the Ontario Ministry of the Environment and warns: "Your private water supply system draws water from a lake or well located in an acid-sensitive area. If water is left stagnant overnight, copper, lead and zinc may accumulate in metal plumbing systems. Since drinking water with high accumulations of lead may cause human disorders, a limit has been developed. . . . Cleansing, by running the tap from which drinking water is being drawn for approximately one minute, will remove accumulations of these metals from the system."

McLennan's voice is angry now. "That's rather sad news when a government simply says, 'Well, we are now in a state of the environment where you can be poisoned, so here's the best we can do for you. We can tell you to avoid this, that and the other thing.' That is definitely bad news. And the other thing that's bad news is the fact that we receive nice booklets from the Ministry of the Environment saying positively do not eat this fish or that fish."

The booklets, in two volumes, are titled *Guide to Eating On-*

tario Sport Fish. There is one for southern Ontario and one for the north. Each booklet is more than 200 pages long—pages filled with tables listing every major water body in the province and assessing the degree of danger from pesticides or from mercury or other metal poisoning facing the heedless fisherman who eats a catch from any one of them. The silhouette of a fish is used as a symbol: A white fish means it's safe to eat the catch, a dotted fish means ten meals a week are permitted, a horizontally striped fish one or two meals per week. A black fish is lethal—forbidden to all those anglers who are not suicidal.

McLennan is exasperated. "Here we are in trout country," he says, "spending millions and millions of dollars stocking a fishery that we think our tourists want and past experience has proven they do, and what our ministry has to say to us is, if there are any fish don't eat them. Or eat limited amounts. For any country or nation to accept that is just about the height of ridiculousness.

"What is really happening is that certain links in the natural food chain are being destroyed. Eventually, the weakest link could break the whole system, and we don't know where that is. Maybe we've reached it now and just aren't aware of it. But when the wild country goes down the tubes the cities, which are mainly brick and mortar, are going with us. Because this is the hinterland, and when the hinterland goes there is no life support system for our cities. And I don't known whether city folk understand that at all."

The symptoms reported by lay people such as McLennan and Mrs. Strath are referred to by scientists as "empirical" evidence, based solely on individual observation and thus lacking the weight of statistically measured samples. Enough scientific studies have been conducted, however, to show that what these ordinary people are seeing does, indeed, fit a pattern—an ominous pattern.

The physical mechanisms that cause destruction and the path of their progress through the aquatic ecosystem are gradually being deciphered as observers build on the pioneer work of early Swedish investigators, of Americans such as Cornell University's Dr. Carl Schofield and of Canadians such as zoologist Dr. Harold Harvey of the University of Toronto.

Schofield, who worked chiefly in the Adirondacks, and Harvey, who labored in the La Cloche region of Killarney Park, Ontario, made many similar observations, documenting sharp drops in both the pH of the water and the fish populations of the lakes they studied.

Harvey became interested in the question in 1967, when he trekked in to Lumsden Lake in the La Cloche mountains to check on the progress of 4,000 pink salmon fingerlings planted there the year before. Lumsden, 60 feet deep in spots, isolated from roads and human settlement and fed by even more isolated headwaters in the remote forest, seemed an ideal environment. Lake trout, perch and herring had prospered there in the past. To Harvey's astonishment, however, the salmon had not prospered. In fact, every single one of them was dead. Subsequent combing of the lake with nets over the next year and a half also showed that the trout, perch and herring were gone, and that a small remnant population of white suckers— the only fish Harvey's team could find—consisted entirely of dwarfed or deformed adults. No young were in evidence. The pH of the water in Lumsden Lake, tested at 6.8 in 1961, had fallen to 4.4 by 1971.

Shocked, Harvey and his research team began checking other lakes in the area and found the same story repeated again and again. At George Lake and OSA Lake the fish had disappeared. Of more than 60 lakes tested in the park watershed, the majority had been affected. A silent tragedy had taken place, almost unnoticed, in the space of a decade.

Its occurrence was of particular significance to Canadians,

for whom the lakes in question have a much more than ordinary cultural value: Killarney's beauty had been the inspiration for the country's first, and greatest, national movement in art—the Group of Seven. These adventurous painters, whose sketching trips to the region in the 1920s produced a body of work uniquely expressive of the Canadian outlook, are one of the nation's glories. The destruction of life in the lakes they painted (OSA stands for Ontario Society of Artists) was a desecration. It was as if, in France, vandals had burned down Lautrec's Moulin Rouge, or sprayed the Provence of Gauguin and Van Gogh with Agent Orange defoliant.

The acid clouds that did the damage had blown south from Inco in neighboring Sudbury, and north from the industrial heartland of the United States.

In New York, meanwhile, Carl Schofield was recording the death of the fish populations of lake after lake in the Adirondacks, especially those at high altitudes where the buffering soil is thin and the plumes from distant smokestacks flow unimpeded. By 1982, 51 percent of all the Adirondack lakes above 2,000 feet in elevation had pH values of less than 5, and 90 percent of these were devoid of fish. The rains that fell on the region averaged pH 4.

Schofield discovered something else. Although a lowering of water pH by itself can alter the body chemistry of fish sufficiently to kill them, many of the fish losses in the Adirondacks were taking place at pH levels normally considered nonlethal. Some other factor had to be at work. That factor, he concluded, was the aluminum, leached from the ground by acid rain and washed into the water. The fish were dying from metal poisoning, especially the toxic effects of aluminum, which coated their gills with a silver sheen. His conclusions were confirmed by subsequent research.

Fish, particularly freshwater fish, are delicately balanced organisms whose metabolism is heavily dependent on the chem-

ical state of the water around them. Like other living creatures, they must maintain an optimum level of nutrients in
their systems and a steady chemical equilibrium within their
body fluids. The salinity of their fluids, for example, must stay
close to 30 percent of that of seawater for survival.

In the oceans, whose waters are more than three times saltier than body fluids, fish are faced with the danger of absorbing too much salinity. Usually the salt is in the form of sodium
chloride, although there are other salts present. The fish must
constantly excrete sodium and chlorine ions. In fresh water,
their problem is the opposite. The fluids of fish in inland lakes
and streams are saltier than the water around them, and they
must fight a never-ending battle to retain sodium. Also requiring constant regulation are the amount of calcium uptake, the
respiration of oxygen and the acid/base balance of their
systems.

The intake and outflow of oxygen, sodium, calcium and the
hydrogen ions that govern acidity is ruled by a process called
"osmoregulation": the regulation of the rate at which the ions
of various elements pass through a fish's cell membranes, particularly those of its gills and gut, via osmosis. Anything that
interferes with this process risks disrupting the basic life functions of the fish, and a serious disruption can be fatal.

Freshwater fishes' cells normally "trade" the hydrogen ions
(H^+) in their blood for sodium (Na^+) ions from the water
around them. If the concentration of hydrogen ions in the
water is increased, which is by definition what happens when
the pH falls, there are proportionately fewer sodium ions to
take up. Fish whose blood is already full of hydrogen ions are
forced to absorb still more hydrogen while finding it harder and
harder to obtain any sodium. The acidity of their blood rises,
and the salt content drops. At pH 5.2 and below, this process
has been shown experimentally to be fatal to brown trout, and
it is probably also lethal to several other trout species.

Other experiments have shown that an increase in hydrogen ions in water can reduce the ability of fish to absorb oxygen through their gills. Mucus forms on the gill tissues at low pH, making gill cells less permeable to oxygen and asphyxiating the fish. Mucus caused by an increase in hydrogen ions forms on the gills of brook trout at pH 4.2. At pH 4.65 white suckers have been shown to experience serious difficulties with calcium regulation, resulting in an increase in the number of fish with deformed spines. Again, the increase in hydrogen ions present in the water at lower pH proportionately decreases the number of available calcium ions.

The fish kills that occur at higher pH levels are probably due to metal toxicity. In laboratory studies, brook trout exposed to synthetic acid solutions and natural Adirondack water with aluminum concentrations above 0.2 milligrams per liter showed a specific toxic response to the aluminum at pH's as high as 5.9. Aluminum ions coat the fishes' gills and prompt the formation of mucus, thus blocking respiration and interfering with the uptake of sodium and other needed elements. Of course, the lower the pH of the rain, the more aluminum will be dissolved from the soil and washed into the lakes and streams.

In springtime in some parts of the Adirondacks, Sweden and Norway, so much aluminum is freed from the soil that it can be seen on the surface of lakes and ponds, a glistening, silvery coat reflecting the rays of the sun.

At pH 5.9, then, fish may be susceptible to aluminum or other metal poisoning; at pH 5.2, to a salt imbalance; at 4.65, to calcium deficiency; and at 4.2, to asphyxiation from loss of oxygen. In the sudden pulses of storms and snowmelts, which can plunge a lake to pH 3.5 or even lower, they may be struck by several effects at once. At different stages in their life cycles—as eggs or fry, for instance—fish may be even more sensitive to damage than they would be as adults. Often a population of adult fish survives an acid pulse, but an entire generation of young may be wiped out. A single ill-timed thunderstorm can eliminate a whole year's crop of trout or salmon.

Similar catastrophes strike the other creatures that live in lakes and ponds. As the pH starts to fall, a progression begins through the aquatic ecosystem, a diary of death marking the gradual ruination of the underwater world.

The progression is not always orderly, in the sense of proceeding neatly from one level in the food chain to another, like fire from a machine gun stitching a straight line. As the pH drops, the damage explodes instead like a series of shotgun blasts, scattering pellets in an irregular but deadly pattern at every species grouping and every stage in the life cycle.

Sometimes the young are hit first, leaving an adult population intact but without replacements. Sometimes a species is not struck directly but diminishes because its food supply has been wiped out. Or a species may actually enjoy a brief heyday of population growth because a predator species that once preyed upon it is gone, only to become moribund later when its own acid tolerance limit is reached. This has been seen with frogs, whose numbers may temporarily rise when some fish species disappear.

The presence of metals in a body of water may accelerate the sequence, while the buffering capacity of a thick humus layer in the soil or of limestone or other calcareous bedrock may slow it. But whatever the situation of an individual lake, in the end there is no sanctuary.

Scientists have found the following steps typical as the numbers move inexorably downward from neutrality to extinction:

At pH 7. Neutral. Positive hydrogen and negative hydroxide ions are in balance.

At pH 6.8. The calcareous shells of clams and snails become thinner than those of their counterparts at pH 7, evidently due to their difficulty in obtaining sufficient calcium ions from the water. The number of calcium ions has become proportionately less as the number of hydrogen ions rises. At this point, subtle shifts may also begin in bacteria populations, whose extremely short life cycles can make them either more vulnerable or more suited to an environmental change. For example, an acid pulse lasting an hour might have no effect on a fish species whose vulnerable spawning stage might have occurred several months ago, but it could wreak havoc among microbes that pass through a delicate growth stage every five minutes. Conversely, due to bacteria's astonishing reproductive speed, an acid-tolerant group could quickly fill in the gap left by the disappearance of another group. The total mass of bacteria remains unchanged, but some groups wax as others wane.

At pH 6.6. The viability of the eggs of the fathead minnow is reduced and fewer of them hatch.

At pH 6.5. The growth rate of brook trout is reduced and lake trout begin to have difficulty reproducing. Among zooplankton, acid-tolerant rotifers start to increase. Filamentous green algae, such as the blooms of *Mougeotia* about which Mrs. Strath complained, make their appearance. Clams and snails become scarcer.

At pH 6. Several species of clams and snails are wiped out and rainbow trout and brook trout populations start to decline. The smooth newt is extinct. Smallmouth bass and walleyes experience reproductive difficulty, as do spotted salamanders. Several species of mayfly cease laying eggs.

At pH 5.8. Tiny crustaceans called copepods (a critical link in the marine food chain) become extinct. Several species of crayfish have trouble regrowing their hard exoskeletons after each molt.

At pH 5.7. Diatoms and yellow and yellow-green algae begin a marked decrease, while filamentous green algae increase.

Many groups, such as *Daphnia*, whose members are physically among the largest plankton, decrease.

At pH 5.5. Rainbow trout and some smallmouth bass populations are extinct, as are fathead minnows. Brook trout, walleye, roach, lake trout and shiners fail to reproduce, and their numbers drop off sharply. Leeches disappear and mayfly larvae vanish.

At pH 5.4. The reproductive ability of most crayfish is impaired.

At pH 5. All snails and most clams are extinct. All but one species of crayfish are extinct. Brook trout, walleye and most bullfrogs are extinct. Atlantic salmon populations decline and most other species of fish experience reproductive difficulty. The total mass of zooplankton available as food for fish begins to drop. Green and blue-green algal "mats" have become widespread; some as thick as four feet lie on the bottom. Insects that can breathe air or that were previously held in check by fish predation experience an upsurge. Water boatmen, water striders and dragonflies, for example, increase. The proportion of fungi in the water increases.

At pH 4.8. Leopard frog numbers decline. A decrease in some species of underwater pondweeds of the *Potamogeton* genus is noted.

At pH 4.5. Mayflies and stoneflies are extinct. A slowing in the overall growth rate and rate of oxygen uptake of bacteria may be noted.

At pH 4.3. Northern pike are extinct and pumpkinseed fish populations decline sharply.

At pH 4.2. The common toad is extinct.

At pH 4. Spring peepers begin to die off. The larvae of the mayfly *Epeorus* will die within 15 to 30 minutes of contacting the water. The oxygen output of *Lobelia* plants declines by 75 percent.

At pH 3.5. Virtually all clams and snails, frogs, fish and crayfish are extinct.

At pH 2.5. Only a few species of acid-tolerant midges, some bacteria and fungi are alive.

At pH 2. Practically speaking, the water is sterile.

Other effects that take place as lakes acidify include an increase in water clarity and a slowing of the rate at which organic matter decomposes underwater. The latter, dubbed the "pickling effect" by journalists, is not fully understood by scientists. Two causes suspected, however, are the disappearance of certain invertebrates, such as snails, that shred organic debris as they feed and also a decrease at low pH in the metabolic rate of decomposition bacteria.

Rocking gently with the current, well-preserved leaves and ferns can be seen clearly on the bottom of acid lakes, even through several feet of water. This remarkable visibility is likely prompted by the absence of certain types of algae and the precipitation of dissolved organic compounds from the water by aluminum. No one is yet certain, however, of the mechanism that causes the unique "acid blue" such lakes take on when viewed from a distance. Small-plane passengers overflying acid lakes notice it immediately. "It's actually beautiful," said one, "like flowers at a funeral."

Also awaiting elaboration are the effects of acidification on bodies of water other than lakes. Both scientists and the popular press have focussed so heavily on dying lakes that rivers, creeks, beaver ponds, reservoirs, streams and the millions of shallow forest pools and springs have often been forgotten. The evidence available, however, suggests that damage to these bodies may also be catastrophic.

The damage to the salmon fisheries in Nova Scotia has already been documented. According to a report presented by Dr. W. D. Watt of the Canadian Department of Fisheries and Oceans at a 1981 conference sponsored by the International Atlantic Salmon Foundation, "approximately 30 percent of the Nova Scotia [salmon] potential is threatened by or already lost to acidification.

"There are nine former salmon rivers with annual mean pH's below 4.7. . . . Their salmon runs are now considered extinct. Another 13 salmon rivers are presently within the pH range 4.7 to 5. In these rivers there are still self-sustaining runs, but their numbers have declined. At the lower end of the range the runs are probably bordering on extinction. There are also nine salmon rivers in the pH range 5.1 to 5.4, which is considered borderline."

The Nova Scotia rivers in question, Watt notes, are "underlaid by hard granitic and metamorphic rocks" and therefore more prone to rapid acidification. Other rivers in areas with more adequately buffered soils are not in such immediate danger. Nevertheless, over the long term even these rivers could be vulnerable. The same is true of salmon rivers in Maine, Quebec and Newfoundland. In Maine and Quebec, a lowering of the pH in several smaller tributaries to major salmon rivers has been observed, and in Newfoundland pH's as low as 5.3 have been recorded in some salmon streams.

The possible demise of such resources must be measured in more than mere pounds of fish lost. Generations of readers of *Field and Stream, Outdoor Life, Sports Afield* and *Outdoor Canada* have regarded a trip to these salmon rivers as the ultimate wilderness fishing experience, a dream for which they are willing to scrimp and save for years. The very names of some streams—such as the Moise or the Ouapetec—stir near-mystical respect among men and women who love the outdoors. The thought that their children, should they travel one day to the north woods, might find these rivers barren is a blow to the soul.

Rivers, of course, are not the only moving waters in danger. It is via small streams and creeks, after all, that the storm waters and snowmelts responsible for acid pulses in lakes arrive. It is along their lengths that the acids rush trapped between narrow banks, still undiluted by the wider waters into which they flow.

Dr. Ronald Hall, a limnologist working with a multidisciplinary Ontario Ministry of the Environment team studying the lakes and streams near Dorset, Ontario, has done a considerable amount of experimental work in the past with moving water environments in both the United States and Ontario. "In streams here [near Dorset] we've measured pH levels as low as 4," he says. "Following a rainstorm the pH may go down one full unit.

"For the past few years we'd been concentrating on spring pH depressions, but then we looked at the data and realized that pH is also depressed in the autumn following the rains, and the effects can be rather severe. Some stream-dwelling organisms may be large in spring and survive the runoff, but they deposit eggs, emerge and just start growing in the fall and that may be the time when they're affected. I have the data to show that there are definitely effects in the fall on insects."

He suspects, while cautioning that proof is still lacking, that periodic acid pulses—rather than a gradual drop in average pH over months or years—may be responsible for the major share of the damage being done to aquatic life, particularly in streams.

"If you look at what goes on in a watershed on an annual basis, as much as 60 to 65 percent of all the water that runs off does so within three months, March, April and May, with as much as 30 to 35 percent during the month of April alone. In a given five-month period most of the pH effects observed in some streams may actually take place within three or four days. It may well be the surges that are affecting things, even over a long-term period."

The story in shallow ponds and small forest pools may also be grim, according to Karen Clark, a scientist who specializes in amphibians. "Amphibians are not really very well studied," she says. "They tend to be neglected when we look at woodland habitats. But studies have shown that in some cases they actually make up more of the biomass [the total physical mass of what's living] of a forest than small mammals or birds. It's because they're not commercially important that they are neglected. But aesthetically they are at least as important as birds."

The surprisingly large proportion of amphibian biomass to the biomass of other life groups in the forest is also an indication that amphibians may play a more important role in the balance of chemical and biological forces than previously realized. Biomass becomes a crucial factor when habitats are examined as whole systems. The so-called "budgets" of various chemicals and compounds, whose passages through a given ecosystem are governed by carefully balanced cycles, can be drastically affected by changes in biomass. In water, for example, a large enough drop in the biomass of the plankton at the bottom of the species pyramid could have a ripple effect resulting in the extinction of larger species at the top.

"Probably 98 percent of amphibians breed in small ponds and shallow forest pools, rather than in large lakes," notes Clark. "In lakes, the pressure from fish predation is too great for them. They also find the small ponds more congenial because, being shallow, they warm up more quickly in the spring when the amphibians breed. Salamanders don't breed at all in lakes. Wood frogs don't. So they rely on these pools.

"And yet these ponds in spring are filled by meltwater from snow which is very acidic. They're filled so fast they have little opportunity to be buffered. We sampled 12 ponds near Plastic Lake, for instance, and 8 of them were below pH 5, some as low as 4.5. Experiments we performed using amphibian egg masses showed that the hatching success of the eggs decreased by as much as 20 to 30 percent between pools at pH 6 and pH 4.5."

The mechanisms by which the eggs are destroyed are insidious: "Studies have shown that acidity affects the hatching enzyme," says Clark. "But there also appears to be a toughening or failure to expand of the membrane around the embryo, so that the embryo when it is ready to hatch can't get out. Normally they would wiggle until they break through, but in the eggs from the acid environment the embryos had been unable to get out and just kept growing. They were wrapped in a tight circle so they couldn't move. Those that did finally get out had deformed spines.

"The presence of aluminum seems to enhance that effect. And then there is something else that happens. At low pH the eggs take longer to hatch, sometimes three or four days longer, and during the delay a fungus often infects the eggs. The growth of the fungus seems to be encouraged by acidity, and the delay in hatching gives it more time to envelop the eggs. The embryos eventually hatch, breaking through the egg membrane, but the long filaments of fungus are there, and they can't get out of the fungus. So they die anyway."

Birds and mammals that depend in part on aquatic habitats have also begun to feel the effects of increasing acidity, both in terms of the loss of favorite food sources and of the increase in toxic metal contamination of those sources that remain. Studies in Sweden have shown a positive correlation between pH of lake water and species richness of fish-eating birds, such as mergansers, loons and gulls.

The diet of the common loon is made up of 80 percent fish and 20 percent crustaceans, molluscs, aquatic insects and leeches—all of which have been shown to be sensitive to acid-ification. In addition, the range of the loon, whose unearthly call has become almost synonymous with the wild north woods, comprises areas whose granitic bedrock is poorly buff-ered. The results seem inevitable, and are already being con-firmed by observation. A 1979 survey in the Adirondacks showed that the loon population there has definitely declined. A 1981 survey in Quebec showed similar occurrences in *la belle province*, where fish-eating mergansers and kingfishers were observed only on lakes whose pH measurements were above 5.6.

Aluminum, mobilized from the soil and concentrated in lake waters at low pH, was suspected of being the causal factor in Swedish studies that revealed reduction of breeding success, lower egg weights and formation of thin, porous eggs among birds near acidic lakes. The aluminum had been absorbed by aquatic insects, which were in turn eaten by the birds.

Among mammals, a 1980 study showed, in the acid-sensi-tive Muskoka/Haliburton region the livers of raccoons con-tained mercury levels of 4.5 parts per million (ppm)—five times higher than the levels in raccoons taken from nonacidi-fied parts of the province. Examination of deer and moose in Sweden have shown higher than normal accumulations of the metal cadmium in the tissues of animals from acidified areas.

In short, the destruction of life in acidifying water systems is not bounded by the shoreline but spreads beyond it, in the air and on land.

The results of acidification, and of efforts to offset it, some-times also take unexpected turns. Liming, for example, is a traditional method of overcoming soil acidity, one that farmers have used for years to balance the pH of their fields. Attempts to raise water pH levels by liming lakes, however, may actually endanger some fish populations. A 1978 study in Sweden indicated that liming could liberate potentially toxic forms of aluminum and thus induce fish kills.

In some lakes it may do more good to add ordinary salt to the water than to add lime. "It's an old adage in fish hatcheries," says biologist Norman Yan. "If the fish are sick, throw salt in the water, because then everything becomes easier for them. They can keep their own body salt at the right level without expending nearly as much energy if there is extra salt in the water. There was a case reported in the Scandinavian scientific literature where they observed that, if they increased the sodium level only slightly, they got a greater increase in fish survival than if they raised the pH from 4 to 5."

The notion that liming is a cure-all that can save acid lakes, eagerly grasped by politicians looking for an easy way to defuse controversy, is largely wishful thinking. To begin with, the cost of liming lakes is quite high, especially when the areas involved are remote. Estimates reported by the U.S. Environmental Protection Agency range from $247 to $500 per metric hectare (2.47 acres). When it is realized that millions upon millions of acres of water would have to be treated, the impracticality of such a scheme becomes obvious.

The lack of efficacy of liming, too, has been made evident by experiments indicating that any beneficial effects due to liming may be only temporary, particularly if the influx of acidity in rain, snow and particulate form continues unabated. From 1973 to 1978, Canadian scientists carried out an extensive program of liming in several acidified lakes near Sudbury, Ontario. Huge quantities of lime and crushed limestone were dumped into the water from boats in an attempt to revivify the lakes. The results were described graphically by authors Ross Howard and Michael Perley in *Acid Rain*:

In August 1976 the ministry dumped 2,500 small bass into Middle Lake, the first step to a restored fishery. The acidity of the water was still well above normal rain and only a bit below neutrality. Conditions appeared right. But by 1977 not one of the fish had survived. Lohi Lake, despite liming up to a near-neutral condition, lost 1,200 added brook trout within four months. Levels of copper in the lake had been rising again, and it was suspected the fish had died of copper poisoning. Undaunted, in 1977 the researchers returned to the lakes with a fresh stock of trout and the ultimate in experimental schemes. They built plastic swimming pools beside a nearby neutral lake and dumped all the trout in there first, to acclimatize them for what came next. The trout were well fed and watered. None died. Then half their number was trucked to Middle and Lohi Lakes. To duplicate the conditions, the half destined for the neutral lake were taken for an equally long and bumpy ride over back roads, and then they too were placed in huge, carefully-constructed submerged cages. At each lake the cages were lowered slowly underwater to avoid sudden temperature changes. Scuba equipped divers were on hand to feed the trout, remove any which died and take water samples. At Middle and Lohi Lakes, the lakes "reclaimed by liming," the divers had short work. Within 24 hours the trout were swimming in confusion, within 48 hours some were dead. At the neutral lake used as comparison, the divers worked all summer feeding healthy fish in their wire cages.

The liming had failed to reduce the toxic metal concentrations in the sediment, and continued acid rainfall had brought new overdoses, washing in more metals from the land and sky. As a senior environment ministry scientist admitted a year later, "liming has at best very limited effectiveness. We lost those lakes and we'll probably have to write them off as dead forever."

Studies launched in Sweden in 1973, although they did not have to contend with the levels of toxic metals present in the Sudbury lakes, also concluded that liming had at best only temporary effect. Wrote Dr. Hans Hultberg of the Swedish Environmental Research Institute, in a report presented at a 1983 conference on acid precipitation: "Liming of acid-stressed ecosystems is, however, not a long-term realistic method of solving the severe integrated effects of acid deposition. It should only be regarded as a countermeasure in valuable aquatic ecosystems awaiting the necessary reduction of acid generating elements at pollution sources." Swedish experimenters, who had noted improvements in lakes treated with lime, warned that once the liming ceased "these changes successively declined due to dilution and continuous acid loading."

The fact is that simple liming, by itself, cannot restore the delicate chemical and biological balance of a system as complex as that of a freshwater lake. Trying to artificially recreate that balance by dumping various substances into the water is a prohibitively expensive and probably hopeless exercise.

Even the mere measurement of the acidity of a lake or stream is a more complex problem than casual observers realize. Maintenance of a steadily high pH level, for example, is no guarantee that a given water body is not losing the battle against acidification. Because any change, up or down, in the concentration of hydrogen ions must be ten times the level of the previous state before it registers as different by one whole number on the pH scale, a considerable deterioration can take place before testers are aware of it. To detect more subtle movement, alkalinity must be measured.

The alkalinity, or acid neutralizing capacity (ANC), of a substance can be compared to the number of dollars in each one of a rich man's numerous bank accounts. The increments on the pH scale are the accounts themselves. A considerable number of dollars can be removed one by one, but not until the last dollar is withdrawn from it will an entire account be closed. In a similar way, the alkalinity or buffering capacity of a lake can be steadily eroded by the loss of carbonates, bicarbonates and hydroxides over a long period, before the account closes and a drop on the pH scale is noted. Scientists, who measure alkalinity in terms of either parts per million (ppm) or milliequivalents per liter, have observed decreases in water alkalinity of up to 70 percent before the pH value of a lake falls appreciably below normal.

It is thus entirely possible that many lakes whose pH measurements currently are high may in reality be bordering on a sudden drop of pH into the acid range. In various regions of the continent, things may be worse than they seem.

The circles of destruction are rippling outward in both Canada and the United States, and as they move they touch many lives:

"I don't think resort or fishing lodge operators are making it known if their fishing has deteriorated," says Dean Wenborn, past president of the Northern Ontario Tourist Outfitters Association. "I know of one operator in particular who bought a resort a few years ago, a fishing resort, based primarily on its proximity to an area that had been well known fishingwise. And now those lakes are almost all devoid of any aquatic life. He personally told me, 'I can't sell fishing in those areas anymore because there just isn't any fishing there.'

"Our association tried to get this fella to be a witness in a class action suit we were thinking of launching against the polluters, but he said, 'No way do I want to get that kind of exposure. That can only hurt my business even worse.' So our position is that we want to create public awareness, but without implying to our customers that it's no longer any use coming up here. It has required a certain balance."

If the meat from the wholesaler is tainted, should the butcher speak out, or get rid of his stock first? The dilemma is not a new one, nor are the lodge owners less than human in repeating the refrain "Don't use my name."

Anonymously, the lodge owners admit the truth: "The most noticeable problem is that the walleye fishery has completely disappeared in this area," said one. "With the heavy acid runoff in the spring, when we get the snowmelt and the fast runoff, it just kills all the spawn. It's halved our business. When you get an inquiry to the lodge that's the first thing they ask you, is have you got a good walleye fishery. If we still had that fishery, and we did $50,000 to $60,000 a year in business, we would be able to double it (to $100,000 or more)."

"Our place is a family business," says another. "My parents started it in the 1940s and I took it over in the 70s. I was born and raised in it. Until the mid-1950s there was no apparent problem. Then about '55 or '56 we were concerned with an algae buildup. The floor of the lake was getting a green slime on it, and the fish quantities went on deteriorating in numbers to the mid-1960s. It was quite difficult to catch any amount of trout.

"Our business took a heck of a jolt. I would say it went down a good 40 percent, maybe 50 percent. My dad became an alcoholic over it and my mom nearly worked herself to death besides. We had to change from a fishing camp to a resort. I started into a bit of lumbering to help sustain the thing and my folks worked in the wintertime wherever they could get jobs. We're going year-round now. We're going heavy into cross-country skiing, which the acid rain doesn't bother. We had to rebuild our cottages for housekeeping cottages. We're far from out of the woods."

"The inland lakes near us are finished," says a third. "The aquatic life in them has pretty much disappeared. We're oriented now to the bay instead, Georgian Bay." To the yachting crowd.

Over the loudspeaker in a bar near the bay, Harry Belafonte is singing "Rum and Coconut Water." Deep-cushioned Swedish modern sofas surround a central fireplace where a birch fire burns. On the tables are magazines—*GAM on Yachting, The New Yorker, Toronto Life*. "Would we cheat an honest sailor?" asks an ad for Genco Sails Limited. "Of course not, you're getting positively the best sail deal anywhere." Outside, along the wooden quai bordering the channel, masts stand in a row, sails furled high over the trim, burnished hulls of the ships they power. Middle-aged men in deck shoes and white duck pants stroll under the trees with plump, tanned women.

Brochures advertising the resort feature pictures of the spacious compound and luxury rooms and speak with unintended irony of "a dazzling complex of coastal waterways. See for yourself why the government has preserved this area for future generations. It's a region so special it had to be saved."

The owner looks his part: tall, tanned, with a mane of wavy white hair. "The people who originally built this place," he says, "a large American corporation, used it as a private customer entertainment resort. They used to fly people here every week from all over North America. They built this very elaborate outpost camp on one of the inland lakes and used it for lake trout fishing and hunting. It was a fly-in setup. There used to be magnificent trout fishing there. And of course that's just totally disappeared.

"Ourselves, we talk to people about renting that camp, and when they raise the question of the fishing we tell them there isn't any and that sort of puts an end to it. If that fishery was still there, our fortune would be made. All our fishing now is out on Georgian Bay. We take charters out. But that's only in summer. If we had the trout it would extend our season to spring and fall."

Instead, there is Harry Belafonte and an ersatz Caribbean on the edge of the north woods.

The summer sportsmen's charters on the bay, now the bedrock of business for an increasing number of lodge owners, have in their turn prompted another effect, this time on the region's commercial fishermen. Hard put to keep their family enterprises out of the red ever since the opening of the Saint Lawrence Seaway brought the lamprey eel to the Great Lakes and decimated the lake trout fishery in the 1950s, the commercial fishermen of Michigan and Ontario are a stubborn breed and used to adversity. Now, however, they face a new threat.

"Since all this acid rain deadened the inland lakes, the sports fishermen have all flocked down to the bay," says 60-year-old Bert Herbert, whose ship *Warren L* operates out of the tiny harbor town of Killarney, Ontario. "They're putting the pressure on, heavy pressure. It's the pickerel they come down for, especially."

Until March 1983 Herbert and his 28-year-old son Stanley worked as partners, sailing out 30 miles into the bay on the *Warren L* and setting their nets for cisco, perch, pike, whitefish and, in October, pickerel. The partnership ended abruptly, explains Herbert, standing alone on the dock in a brown work shirt and pants, looking worn and tired. "Stanley drowned in March. There was a fella out ice fishing and he went through the thin ice. Stanley jumped on a snowmobile to go out to save him and the snow machine reversed. It came back on him and he went through. I damn near sold 'er after it happened. It was the biggest funeral ever held in Killarney. People came from all over.

"He was a hell of a good fisherman. It was him, when the whitefish market went all to nothing, who came up with the idea to have a fish and chip wagon. That wagon's pulled us through a lot of tight spots since the fishery's been in decline.

"It's getting harder all the time. As the sports fishermen come down, we get pushed farther and farther out into the bay. The Ministry of Natural Resources excludes us from the sports fishing spots. It states on our license that our areas are restricted and we have a quota of what we can catch. We'd love to fish the shoreline. In the old days we did. But that's where the sports fishermen want to go now. The perch, bass, pike and pickerel they want spawn inshore, unlike the lake trout and chubb that spawn in deep water. But the ones that spawn in-shore, in the shallower depths, are affected by the acid rain. It bothers their young. Their numbers are down.

"On top of that the sports fishermen throw things off balance. They only take the sport and predator fish, and leave all the so-called 'garbage' species, the rock bass and suckers, to multiply until they crowd everything. When we fished inshore we took everything, carp, suckers, everything. It was balanced fishing and no one group got undue pressure. Our pickerel quota now is next to nothing. We can fill it in two lifts of the net. If a farmer plants a garden and doesn't pull the weeds, pretty soon he's got no garden."

His face darkens in a scowl. "There's other things go on. There's a police post here in town and just lately the cops went and pulled one fella's nets right out of the water. They said they were illegal nets, because they weren't marked. But they were marked. Some damn tourist operator or sports fisherman went and cut the marker jugs off of them because they knew what the police would do. We had to get hold of our member of Parliament to straighten that out."

There are tales and rumors of other confrontations, of shouted threats, in some cases fights, when charterboats full of sports-men meet commercial boats out in the Great Lakes. To kill the rumors and defuse hard feelings, user group meetings are now held in which sports and commercial fishermen get together to settle problems amicably.

Such meetings would likely not be necessary if the inland lakes were still alive. The ripples spread outward.

Hundreds of miles away, near Big Moose Lake in northern New York, retired state forest ranger Bill Marleau stands on his front lawn, his hands in his pockets. He has only been retired for a few weeks and, though the insignia have been removed, still wears the olive drab uniform jacket and pants that were the mark of his profession for 35 years.

He is 61 now, and has time to remember:

"Any water that's so bad it will dissolve copper or aluminum screening in less than two months, is that good? Is it healthy?" he asks. "Do you know what an Indian Pump is, for fighting forest fires? It's a water can that a crewman carries on his back fighting the fire. You fill 'em with water, they weigh about 75 pounds and they have a hand pump on them. Where you fill it there's a little screen in there so you don't get dirt in that little hand pump, and the screen is copper.

"Well my water pipes froze up, so I went up to Twitchell Creek and filled about ten of these with water to use till I fixed the pipes. After I fixed them I left some of these cans in the cellar. In less than two months there was nothing left of those little screens but about a half-inch of the rim. They were completely dissolved. The pH of the water from Twitchell Creek is just a little over 4, and that used to be one of our better trout streams here in the Adirondacks.

"Where I have my camp at Woods Lake it was excellent fishing once. There's nothing in it at all now. The last trout was caught in 1969. It's very clear. All the vegetation [in the water] has died. There's no bird life or insect life around it, or anything. When I was a kid, right down here by the railroad station there were sometimes a couple hundred swallows lined up to go south in the fall. They lined up on the telephone wires, and down by McKeever at one time there must have been close to a thousand swallows on the wires. Now there are hardly any. There were four out here, two pairs, all summer long at the railroad station.

"Maybe it isn't all due to acid rain, but what is causing it? There aren't any mayflies left, or darning needles. They were all over. Every body of water you went to was full of darning needles before. Yesterday we took a hike to a lake that's back about five miles in the woods. It's a real wilderness lake. We walked back there and we saw one old deer track. We got in to the lake and we ate our lunch and we heard one blue jay and we saw one darning needle and that's the total wildlife we saw on a ten-mile walk through nothing but wilderness that used to be teeming with life when I was young. There were dead trees and bushes all over the trail. You couldn't hear any bird life. Oh yes, I saw one junco. On the way out we heard one junco." Marleau's voice is bitter now. His fist clenches.

"But that's pitiful! I mean, I was born right here in this town and I've lived here all my life except for three years in the Navy in World War II, and I've hunted and fished and was a forest ranger 35 years, and I *know* what it was like when I was a kid! I know what it was like 40 years ago and 30 years ago and 20 years ago. And I know when I was a kid it wasn't like it was when my father was a boy. And when I got to be 22 it wasn't like it was when I was a kid—but it was still doggone good!

"I had a Boy Scout troop and today they're all grown men with their own children and if they see me, they ask me 'Are the bullfrogs still chunking up there at Woods Lake like they used to?' They used to put up a solid chorus there so that you couldn't sleep, and the kids would get mad and yell and the frogs would shut up, but only for a couple of minutes. So they ask, are they still there, and I have to say no, they're not.

"And I wonder. What's going to be left for my grandchildren?"

Three

No One Knows Why

The farmers of the *bois-francs* hills don't like to waste things, even words. Their lives have been merged for generations with soil, crops, animals and trees—with basics—to the point where only the basic seems worth talking about. Short sentences suffice, at least with strangers. André Marcoux, 28 years old with a wife and child, is typical. He has just been wiped out, financially ruined, but the flood of angry, emotional words one would expect in the face of such a blow does not come. Instead, there is silence, broken only when a direct question is asked and courtesy requires a response.

Dressed in a T-shirt and jeans, a welder's cap on his head, the dark-haired young farmer sits on a pile of logs and looks around him at the huge opening in the forest. The logs on which he sits, cut with a chainsaw into stove-size lengths, are all that remain of the majestic stand of sugar maple trees, some of them 80 to 100 years old, that only recently shaded the fields on every side.

"*C'est une perte totale*—a total loss," Marcoux says, his polite International French phrases tinged with the accent of the *joual* dialect of rural Quebec in which he is more at ease. "It took us a year to cut it all down, my brother Jacques and I. It came to 3,300 full cords of firewood. We found buyers for 3,000, so there's about 300 cords left to sell.

"The auction is next Tuesday, for the farm. We're selling our animals and machinery, all the sugar-making equipment too. Forty cows we'll sell. Holsteins, good milking cows. We took out a loan from the Fiducie du Quebec to buy the sugaring equipment—$112,000 we paid for the tubing and every-thing—and we have to make the payments just the same."

André and his brother Jacques, 32, also married and the fa-ther of a child, bought the dairy farm in which they have been partners in 1976. They knew what they were getting, that it was a good farm, because they had grown up there. It has been the home and source of livelihood of the Marcoux family for 45 years. "My father had it before us and before him my grand-father," says André.

But only three years were needed to destroy it.

"We started with 20 cows," Jacques Marcoux says, taking up his younger brother's tale. "They were good producers and we grew little by little until we had 40 head. Then we started to tap the sugar bush. My father had done it and my grandfather and so we decided to tap. The first year we had a good year. We put in 5,000 taps and made 55 barrels of maple syrup."

Optimism must have run high after that first success. The brothers had made $20,000 net on their syrup, more than what they cleared after expenses on their dairy operations, and decided to go into the sugar business in earnest. They bought all-new sugaring equipment, evaporators and plastic tubing, and the next spring put in 6,000 more taps. They expected a bonanza that would pay for their investment and launch them on the road to prosperity. Neither of them thought much about the small number of trees in their bush that had mysteriously died in that first year of an inexplicable "disease," a malady that caused its victims to exhibit all of the symptoms of drought in the midst of abundant rain. First, the leaves at the top of each tree browned and died, then the branches of the crown. The damage moved from the top down until the whole length of the tree was affected and all of its leaves were shed—in August.

That first year, less than 10 percent of the maple stand was hit, and not all of the stricken trees died.

In the second year of tapping, however, there was no bonanza. There was disaster. "We had 11,000 taps in," says Jacques. "But that year 30 percent of our trees were hit by the disease and we only produced 35 barrels of syrup. More than double the taps but less than half the output. The first year was the only good year we had. By the third year 85 to 90 percent of the trees were hit and we only produced 16 barrels of syrup. Now it's finished. They're all gone, 100 percent."

The tone of Marcoux's voice is laconic, matter-of-fact, but the look in his eyes gives his feelings away: It says, "What happened?" He is astonished. He has been sawing and stacking the trunks of the great trees for a full year, laboring winter and spring, and cannot understand why. After 45 years, all at once, every tree is dead, he and his brother are broke, and the auction is Tuesday.

"In three years," says André, echoing his brother's astonishment, "all gone. And no one knows why."

Just up the road from the Marcoux farm is the white frame house of their neighbor Robert LaFlamme, also a farmer and the proprietor of a sugar bush. Sitting at his kitchen table, an empty cup in front of him like a symbol of the future, LaFlamme admits his own bush may soon follow the Marcoux brothers' maples into oblivion:

"It's not as bad yet, but it's continuing," he says. "I've lost 500 out of 2,000 trees and I calculate if it continues at the same rate, in three or four years there'll be just about nothing left. I have 30 head of Holsteins and they're our principal source of revenue. But the maples, since we've been on the land we've tapped them, and some years it's just with them that we manage to make it. They're important. I'm a farmer, and I live by these things."

Like his neighbors, LaFlamme bought his farm from his father—25 years ago. Every day, seven days a week, he milks his herd, and every spring for a quarter of a century he has tapped his maples. He refers to the disease that is killing them as *"la sécheresse"*—drought—even though there is no drought, because the symptoms shown by the trees are those of dryness. *"Ça séche,"* he says, "they dry. They've been drying up here for three years now."

He discounts newspaper claims that the losses, widespread not only in the *bois-francs* region but also in the *Beauce* and the townships bordering Vermont, are due to poor management practices on the part of the sugar bush owners, that the recent introduction of vacuum pumps and plastic tubing and consequent intensive extraction of sap has overstressed the trees.

"Me, I don't have any vacuum pumps, and the trees are drying out just the same. I even have some parts of the bush that aren't tapped, that aren't hooked up to the tubing, and they dry anyway. It's impossible to say that the pump and tube tapping method has done this. Besides, if people do use pumps, there are some who've been using them for 15 years and their trees never dried."

He raps his cup on the table top: *"Il y a des gars qui ne font pas pantout, mais ça séche pareil!"* There are guys who don't tap at all, and they dry just the same. . . .

"They don't know what's doing it. The government is doing studies. The Marcoux brothers told me the government guys say it's a lack of lime in their sugar bush. But the bush has been there for 150 years, 150 years those trees have been growing, and more, and they never have been limed. And now, all in one blow, they're all dried up. It's impossible. They didn't need lime. Something else is doing it. I can't tell you what, but it's not any damn lack of lime!"

The Quebec government, surprised by the losses in a provincial industry whose production is worth more than $30 million at the wholesale level alone, has assigned a team of scientists from the Ministry of Energy and Resources to make a diagnosis of the "disease." A group of technicians, toting clipboards and wearing orange hard hats, had been on the site that morning, taking soil samples and measuring tree diameters in local sugar bushes, including the remnants of the Marcoux woodlot. A formal report is expected in about two years, but the technicians admit "nobody knows yet what the trouble is."

The name of the mysterious doom overtaking the maple syrup producers of Quebec is not yet part of the vocabulary of New France.

Unfortunately, the dying of the trees is not limited only to Canada's French-speaking province. Similar phenomena are taking place elsewhere. And in Germany, Poland, Czechoslovakia and Scandinavia, in New Hampshire and Vermont the silent killer of forests has been given a name:

"Bonn will combat acid rain," announced the headline in the *Suddeutsche Zeitung* of September 2, 1982. The West German federal cabinet had decided to draft new regulations for the control of sulphur dioxide emissions from fossil-fuel-burning power plants, and the regulations would be strict. According to the Ministry of the Interior, SO_2 emissions would be limited to 400 milligrams per cubic meter of stack gases. Existing power stations would be required to meet the limit within ten years. Any plants whose owners believed they could not be converted to meet the goal would be forced to shut down permanently in five years.

In a press release accompanying the cabinet announcement, the interior ministry's intentions in pressing for new rules were explained: "The principal goal of the new measure is control of the acid rain phenomenon. In a public statement, [Interior Minister] Baum described the connection between sulphur emission, acid rain and forest damage as unequivocal and emphatically rejected arguments heard from industry sources that the cause of tree damage had not been sufficiently investigated. He emphasized that environmental policy decisions cannot be delayed until the complete chain of cause and effect leading to soil acidification is elucidated. The matter must be dealt with now."

Such resolution on the part of any politician could not spring up in a vacuum, and that of German officialdom was no exception. The decision came only after sharp debate in the federal cabinet, a debate that was itself prompted by heavy pressure from inside and outside government ranks. A year earlier, a series of articles in the popular newsmagazine *Der Spiegel* had stirred a public outcry. According to the magazine, an epidemic of destruction was attacking German forests, causing massive tree dieback across the country. Trees everywhere were threatened, including the famed Black Forest, the Hartz Mountains and the timbered hills of Bavaria. Articles in other publications, such as the respected environmental magazine *Natur*, repeated similar warnings, and the German people, who regard their forests with a degree of respect unusual even among lovers of nature, were profoundly shocked.

Even more shocking for the government were the results of a survey authorized in November 1981 by a conference of federal representatives and provincial environment ministers. The survey, conducted by a committee of scientists and government delegates chaired by the federal Minister of Food, Agriculture and Forestry, was based on reports from the forestry offices of each *Länder* (province). Although it was not made public until November 1982, its preliminary findings undoubtedly influenced the September cabinet announcement. The formal report, titled *Forest Damage Due to Air Pollution*, was framed in conservative terms and even so was frightening in its implications:

> The *Länder* report a total stricken area of approximately 560,000 hectares [1,385,000 acres]; this means that 7.7 percent of the forest area in the Federal Republic of Germany is affected.
>
> When interpreting these figures it must be remembered that incipient damage of this type is difficult to recognize and, to a large extent, underestimated or overlooked. Furthermore, thinned damaged trees from stands being thinned are not usually declared. It must also be taken into account that for individual species only the reduced damage area was surveyed; in other words, for a mixed stand with an area of ten hectares where the fir accounts for 33 percent and shows signs of damage, only 3.3 hectares were recorded. In practice, however, this means that the entire ten hectare stand is significantly affected.
>
> It must also not be forgotten that emission damage has been noted for a large number of years in industrialized areas. Such areas are not included in damage reports.

In short, the 7.7 percent damage figure actually recorded was probably a gross underestimate of what had really happened, and worse was yet to come. The picture became even more serious when the damage was looked at species by species, rather than across the board: "Fir is the most severely damaged species. Approximately 60 percent of the area covered by fir is affected. Spruce is the next most severely affected species; it follows a long way behind fir (approximately ten percent of the area covered by spruce) but at the same time well ahead of other damaged species."

Five percent of the nation's pines were also stricken; and fir, spruce and pine are the three species of greatest economic importance to the country's forest industry.

A second survey in 1983, by the same committee, produced even more terrible results. In the single year between surveys the damage increased four times, leaving a total of 2.5 million hectares (6.1 million acres)—or one third of all of Germany's forests—stricken. The later damage report noted that 41 percent of the nation's spruce, 43 percent of its pine forests and 76 percent of its white fir trees were injured, as well as 26 percent of the country's beech woodlands.

The authors of these surveys make no bones about the cause of this disaster: "It has been confirmed that, in addition to regionally restricted, easily explicable forest damage (e.g., pest epidemics, climate and weather), there is also forest damage which cannot be explained solely on the basis of causes known so far. . . . There are indications that atmospheric pollutants and their conversion products are a major cause of forest damage; sulphur dioxide is probably the most important."

Such reports in many ways confirmed the work of German scientists who had been studying the effects of acid deposition on forests since the early 1960s, and especially the work of Dr. Bernhard Ulrich of the Institute for Land Resources and Forestry at the University of Göttingen. All but ignored by North Americans before 1980, Ulrich's work was introduced to the United States and Canada through the efforts of Canadian wood chemist and retired Domtar vice-president of research Dr. George Tomlinson, who summarized and interpreted it in articles published in North America.

Ulrich had summarized his own findings in a 1980 paper whose cumbersome title translates as *The Predicted Development of the Forests of Central Europe Based on a Study of Environmental Pollution and the Associated Theoretical Risks.* Noting that continent-wide emissions of sulphur dioxide, stable from 1910 to 1950, had doubled between 1950 and 1972, he reported that an area of permanent pollution had been formed in central Europe, where the mean pH of rainfall had dropped to 4.1.

At the time Ulrich began his research in the mid-1960s, most scientists believed that the greatest damage to trees from SO_2 was caused by direct contact of the gas with exposed leaf surfaces, and that below a given aerial concentration these effects were minimal or even nonexistent. Those beliefs, Ulrich's work helped to show, were only partially true. Of course, sulphur dioxide in its gaseous form does cause leaf injury. As the authors of the Canadian National Research Council report *Sulphur and Its Inorganic Derivatives in the Canadian Environment* note, "Chronic and acute injuries to vegetation by SO_2 are reflected as characteristic visual symptoms or markings of the foliage. . . . In general chronic injury shows as a chlorosis. The cells are not killed but the chlorophyll is bleached; in some cases a silvering of affected areas occurs, but in others a yellowing or bronzing appears. Leaves often age prematurely and are shed. Acute injury kills the cells in the interveinal and sometimes distal areas of the leaf. Here metabolic processes cease."

It is also true that the foliar effects are greater at higher SO_2 concentrations, and that the lower the concentration the less marked are the short-term effects on the plant. But Ulrich, as well as other researchers monitoring forest damage, soon realized that the assumption by earlier observers that a "no-damage threshold" existed below which tissue injury from SO_2 could not occur was largely wishful thinking. Observations in Czechoslovakia in 1973 and Germany in 1979 showed that tree damage was in fact taking place in areas where atmospheric concentrations of SO_2 were well below the assumed "safe" thresholds. In 1982, the International Union of Forest Research Organizations decided that there was no safe limit.

By the late 1970s, researchers had also begun to realize that the deposition of both solid particles and the acidic liquid products of SO_2 and NO_x were as destructive as gaseous pollution and that their effects might be cumulative, resulting in progressive degradation over a long term even where short-term effects had not been detectable.

Ulrich's examinations of the Solling forest and soils led him to two further conclusions. First, he determined, the acid load striking many forests was much higher than previously believed, and, second, the mechanism by which the most lethal damage was being done involved not foliage, but the *root systems* of trees.

The higher acid loading of forests compared to that of open fields is due to the filtering abilities of the forest canopy, which captures pollutants in whatever form they appear: as gaseous SO_2 or in acidic aerosols and fog. Aerosols, consisting of minute particles of sulphuric and nitric acids and their salts, which make polluted air hazy, are deposited on leaf surfaces and bark as they pass through the upper branches of a stand of trees. Gaseous SO_2 is also taken up by both bark and foliage, and it is oxidized by the metabolism of the trees themselves into sulphuric acid. When an acid rainstorm later occurs, the accumulated burden of acidity from all sources is washed off, and flows along with the rain down the trunks to the forest floor. Thus the ultimate acid concentration reaching the soil is much higher than what the acid rain alone could produce.

This filtering effect of the air by trees is greater in evergreen forests, which keep their needles year-round, than in deciduous woods. Hardwood stands, because they shed their leaves each fall, take in only a fraction of the acid dose endured by conifers. Ulrich's measurements in the Solling region of Germany showed that in beech forests the rain striking the canopy was only 58 percent as acidic as the total burden reaching the forest floor. In spruce forests, the rain itself contributed only 26 percent of the acidity that ultimately reached the ground. Trees located on the windward side, usually the western slopes, of hills and mountains also tended to receive heavier doses, with the comparison in this case to either the windward trees' lowland counterparts or to stands located in the lee of the prevailing winds.

The root-system impacts described by Ulrich were startling but logical: "The increase in acidity shows up in the chemical parameters of the soil in the form of a drop in the pH value and the occurrence of toxic concentrations of aluminum in the soil solution," he wrote in his summary paper. "The presence of aluminum in the soil solution triggers a drastic decline in the viable fine root biomass from 2,500 kilograms per hectare to a few hundred kilograms."

Such a decline was remarkable in itself, but Ulrich found that the effects continued: "If the soil is not able to buffer the increased acidity quickly enough, then after the short [fine] roots, the long roots are also damaged. This can initiate a fateful course of development. Damaged long roots retain their function as conduits supplying the current of water required for transpiration, but they no longer exert any control over the substances that are taken up in the soil solution. If the solution is acidic, the aluminum that is contained in the bark of all roots may be mobilized and large sections of the root system, including roots several inches thick, may die off. This danger increases with the intensity of the upsurge in acidity."

In other words, poisoned by the aluminum freed from soil clays by the acidification of the soil water, the roots of a forest are gradually choked off, cutting the flow of moisture and nutrients to trunks, branches and leaves.

This process is accelerated still further by a multitude of other effects. For example, the ability of leaves to buffer the direct consequences of contact with acid aerosols and gaseous SO_2 is dependent on their ability to exchange the incoming hydrogen ions with calcium ions stored in their tissues. Ulrich noted that in acid soils "the roots contain small amounts of calcium and large amounts of aluminum." Magnesium and other essential nutrients in the soil are also constantly being leached away. Thus less calcium is available to be transferred from the roots to the leaves, where it is needed as a buffer, while the load of toxic aluminum ions continues to increase, so that the tree is starved of other basic nutrients as well.

Roots that are damaged, and therefore less disease resistant, also allow the entrance of bacteria that cause a condition known as "wet wood." This disease reduces the tree's ability to conduct water to its upper branches, thus accentuating the already drought-like effects of the loss of the fine roots. As if that weren't enough, the lack of available calcium also interferes with the process of lignification—the manufacturing of wood—in affected trees, while the destruction of leaf surfaces by acid damage opens the way to epidemics of insect infestation.

Finally, the loss of the fine root systems weakens the trees' ability to remain upright. As Ulrich wrote: "If the short roots are dead, the long roots can be pulled out of moist soil like threads. Therefore, root-damaged trees are less securely anchored in the soil and are thus prime candidates for being thrown down by the wind. . . . The major [European] storm catastrophe of 1972 was not just a result of the stormy conditions, but also was due to root damage that had occurred beforehand over a large area, as was discovered in the Solling Mountains in 1969."

In sum, what Ulrich was describing was a whole series of interconnected and mutually reinforcing disasters whose combined weight was overwhelming. Few susceptible forests could prevail when pitted against them, especially not stands of fir growing on thin, acid soils at high elevations where they were already exposed to continual stress from cold and wind.

Ulrich's observations included descriptions of what may be the classic symptoms of acid damage, in individual trees as well as at the level of the forest itself. As Tomlinson outlined it in a 1982 report to Domtar, written after discussing the data with Ulrich, the destruction of the fine roots of each tree is followed by "a premature loss of needles or leaves, normally preceded by discoloration, followed by necrosis (localized death of living tissue) of the bark, twigs and branches, particularly in the crown. The moisture content of the tree becomes abnormally low even though the soil may contain adequate moisture. The growth rate slows and following an extended period often lasting many years, the tree may die."

In his 1980 paper, the German scientist himself described the damage's progress through a forest: "The edges of forests are subject to extremely severe pollution because they intercept large quantities of SO_2. In the areas where pollution occurs the trees sustain leaf and shoot damage and as a result the closed edge of the forest breaks down. Because of the vertical interception of SO_2 that now penetrates to the interior of the stand, it is no longer possible to stabilize this edge once it has been opened up.

"The acidification of the soil increases so quickly in the edge zone that new trees are continuously drying out and falling or being thrown down. In this way, the damage eats its way further into the forest like a malignant growth."

Already stressed by the effects of acidity, weakened trees lack resistance and fall prey to insect, fungus and bacterial infections as well. Storms and periods of adverse weather that would pose no problems to a healthy stand may wreak havoc among trees in an acidified environment. (Under the extra stress of being tapped, maple trees may suffer additionally.)

Ulrich's conclusions are still controversial among some scientists, who disagree with one or another detail of the picture presented, but the overall import of the data he and others had amassed was impossible for the West German government to ignore. Similar observations were also being reported from

Eastern Europe. In Poland, for example, Jerzy A. Lesinski of the Department of Forest Ecology of the Agricultural University at Cracow noted that more than 600,000 hectares (1,485,148 acres) of forest were "severely damaged" by air pollution in 1980, with the damage following the typical top-down pattern.

As Agatha Christie might have put it, there were no eyewitnesses to the crime and no confession, but the body was there and the circumstantial evidence was compelling.

In North America, the same kinds of symptoms are being reported with increasing frequency in New York, New England and Eastern Canada. In Vermont, scientists from the University of Vermont and Yale University have been monitoring forest losses in the Green Mountains for several years. Yale's Dr. Thomas Siccama, in a 1982 paper co-authored by the University of Vermont's Margaret Bliss and Dr. Hubert Vogelmann, and published in the *Bulletin of the Torrey Botanical Club*, documented the decline of red spruce over a period of 15 years at Camels Hump, near Huntington, Vermont, and at sites on Bolton Mountain and Jay Peak. Declines in stand density ranged from 27 percent to 93 percent, depending on the elevation of the stand and the size class of tree being surveyed. By 1979, the density of standing dead spruce at Camels Hump exceeded that of the living trees. Although actual death of balsam fir stands was not noted in the area, the probability that this species also was suffering was indicated by a slowing of growth as measured by trunk ring widths.

"The characteristic pattern of death of red spruce is a general browning and loss of needles from the crown apex downward and from the terminals of lateral branches inwards over several to many years," wrote Siccama. "This pattern seems to hold for large old trees 30 meters tall as well as saplings 2 meters tall in the shrub stratum. These symptoms are typical of death due to drought stress."

After explaining that neither drought nor infestations of such pests as spruce budworm had occurred, the paper noted that "exceptionally low pH of forest floor humus" had been reported in forests both north and south of Camels Hump and that "acid rain is leaching manganese, calcium, magnesium, potassium and zinc" from the soil. "The general pattern of death, symptoms of water stress, may be due not to lack of soil moisture but to some sort of root damage," it concluded.

A decline of spruce stands following the same pattern has also been recorded in the Adirondack Mountains in New York (as has been documented by D. J. Raynal *et al.* in 1980) and at the Hubbard Brook Experimental Forest in the White Mountains of New Hampshire between 1965 and 1977 (unpublished). The most impressive body of evidence, however, in the form of both field studies and controlled laboratory experiments where field conditions are duplicated, has been marshalled by the group of scientists working with Vermont's Dr. Vogelmann at Camels Hump. Ironically, a large part of the funding for this group was initially provided by a grant from American Electric Power, owners of the infamous Gavin plant discussed earlier. AEP's funding ceased in 1983, after Vogelmann published a general account of what he was finding in an article in *Natural History* magazine.

"It's the same thing as the old cigarette smoking/lung cancer controversy," Vogelmann says. "No matter how much material is accumulated, somebody in the tobacco industry will always say that statistically you haven't proven it. *Perfectly* unequivocal proof of a causal link between acid precipitation and tree dieback is lacking and probably always will be. The complexity of the natural environment is so great that it would be difficult to say that beyond doubt acid rain is responsible for everything we've observed.

"But there is a lot of experimental evidence that we have that points in that direction. A lot of it."

What researchers have seen at Camels Hump was described movingly by Vogelmann in his November 1982 article in *Natural History*:

> Twenty years ago the evergreen forests on the slopes of Camels Hump, a high peak in the northern Green Mountains of Vermont, were deep green and dense. The red spruces and balsam firs that dominated the vegetation near the mountaintop thrived. . . . The trees were luxuriant, the forest was fragrant, and a walk among the conifers gave one a feeling of serenity— a sense of entering a primeval forest.
>
> Today the red spruces are dead or dying and some firs look sick. Gray skeletons of trees, their branches devoid of needles, are everywhere in the forest. Trees young and old are dead, and most of those still alive bear brown needles and have unhealthy looking crowns. Craggy tops of dead giant spruces are silhouetted against the sky. The brittle treetops often break off, leaving only a jagged lower trunk with a few scraggly branches. Strong mountain winds overthrow many dead trees, tipping upward their shallow root systems along with chunks of the forest floor. As more and more trees die and are blown down, the survivors have less protection from the wind, and even they are toppled over. The forest looks as if it has been struck by a hurricane.

Noting that spruce-fir forests at 3,500 to 4,000 feet are already growing in a stressful environment, including "a severe subarctic climate with a short growing season and soils that are thin, nutritionally depauperate and naturally acidic," Vogelmann warned that the higher-elevation forests may get twice as much precipitation as trees at lower elevations and that the acid load at the higher elevations "is more than doubled, and so is the dose of toxic heavy metals."

Laboratory experiments at the University of Vermont, he added, have "demonstrated that exposure to either acid rain or a heavy metal will stunt plants, but when the two are combined (in the form of acidified water to which small amounts of aluminum, copper, lead or zinc have been added) all plants show sharp declines and the result can be lethal, suggesting a strong synergistic effect." Core samples drilled from the trunks of spruce trees as old as 200 years of age, he said, have been analyzed chemically and show a sharp upswing in the concentration of potentially toxic aluminum beginning around 1950— when increases in the acidity of rainfall in the area were first noted.

Like Ulrich in Germany, the Vermont group also suspects that aluminum may be causing the greatest damage, by destroying the fine roots of affected trees. "An experiment carried out in our laboratory demonstrates that spruce trees growing in acidified water to which small amounts of aluminum or cadmium have been added do indeed show a reduction in water uptake. The laboratory plants soon take on the look of the dying spruces in the forest."

Spruce and fir weren't the only species affected, either, Vogelmann wrote. "From 1965 to the present the basal areas [a measurement of standing tree volume] of sugar maple and beech growing on the lower slopes of Camels Hump dropped significantly, those of maples by 15 percent and the beeches by 30 percent. The number of maple seedlings and saplings dropped 57 percent."

In an interview, he noted that core samples have also been taken from maples and that a "very sophisticated" analysis of one sugar maple core was particularly striking. "The pattern of uptake of aluminum by the spruce in the last 30 years is very real," he said. "And this has been verified—by a different laboratory—with the sugar maple core we had analyzed. It showed the very same pattern: a slowdown in growth starting about 30 years ago, with a [simultaneous] uptake of aluminum. It matches beautifully with the red spruce. The pattern is just a perfect overlap."

The mounting evidence that damage is not limited to spruce, or even to evergreens in general, is ominous, he added. "It's possible these trees [on Camels Hump] may be like the miners' canary, which was more vulnerable to poison gases than the miners themselves. Its death was a warning that they were next. The effects we see now may eventually spread to trees on more favorable sites."

In his progress reports to American Electric Power Service Corporation (a subsidiary of American Electric Power Company), Vogelmann discussed not only the core samples and on-site tree surveys but numerous other experiments that were mounted and the effects observed by members of his group. For example, Yale's Dr. Siccama, whose original surveys of the Camels Hump flora in the mid-1960s provided the data base against which later measurements could be compared, had included mosses in his observations. A second tour, in 1979, of the same area and in some cases the identical sites, showed "profound reductions in moss coverage": in some cases to less than half the former surface covered.

In addition to this survey, specimens of a common moss from the area (*Polytrichum ohioensis*) were grown in the laboratory, where they were subjected to low pH levels and various concentrations of aluminum and other metals. According to Vogelmann's report, the results indicated that "*P. ohioensis* growth is reduced by low pH and that the interaction between low pH and metals is particularly repressive to growth."

Field observations in 1965 and 1981 also showed that litter (such as fallen leaves, needles and branches) on the forest floor had "increased by a factor of 3–4, indicating that litter decomposition has been drastically reduced." If litter does not decompose, of course, the nutrients that it contains and that are essential for plant growth will not be made available for roots to take up. Like the "pickled" leaves in an acidified lake, the leaves and detritus of the forest will simply pile up, uselessly, nourishing nothing.

Vogelmann noted that laboratory work indicated "the metabolism of litter-degrading microorganisms was reduced by low pH and was further reduced when lead and zinc ions were present. These results suggest that microbially caused litter decomposition may be altered by acidic, metal-containing precipitation."

Apparently, these were not the kind of results American Electric Power was looking forward to when it decided to fund the University of Vermont group, nor was the Vogelmann article in *Natural History* the sort of publicity that would be appreciated by a utility anxious to dispel suspicions that emissions from its smokestacks could damage the environment.

In a 5 November 1982 letter to Vogelmann, AEP assistant vice-president R. W. Reeves complained: "Upon reading your recent article in *Natural History*, I found many of your statements . . . as well as the general tone of the piece to be deeply disturbing. . . . I believe many of the claims in the article to be unsupported." Noting that he did not dispute the "basic premise" that the red spruce on Camels Hump are in decline, he added that "the clear implication of your *Natural History* article is that this decline can be directly linked to acid rain and heavy metal deposition. In contrast, the results you have reported (in annual progress reports to the company) have almost all been described as preliminary or very preliminary, leaving any link between the spruce decline and acid rain/metal deposition as extremely circumstantial."

After objecting to a number of minor differences in wording between the magazine article and Vogelmann's other written reports, Reeves focussed on what was obviously the real source of AEP's anxiety: "Your discussion of general theories on the causes of acid rain is very simplistic and misleading. There is absolutely no sound scientific support for the claim that acid rain began to occur in the 1950's, and in fact a strong case can be made for its existence long before this time. The same is true regarding claims of the increasing geographical extent of acid rain. Also, the picture you paint of the Midwest causing acid rain in New England completely ignores the increasing evidence that local, short-range sources may be playing as important a role as long-range transport in contributing to acid deposition. There are more misconceptions in your article, but I hope you see my point."

The point, of course, was as obvious as a pimple on the queen's nose. Vogelmann's reply, on 15 November, was polite but blunt. Reminding Reeves that nearly six months had passed between his last progress report to AEP and the production of the magazine article, months in which "research activity, some of which formed part of the article," had been ongoing, Vogelmann labelled the letter's criticism of several points "matters of syntax and semantics rather than of substance."

He denied that the article was misleading, pointing out that numerous "notes of caution" had been included in the text to warn readers that its statements were not meant to be taken as categorical and that the findings had been honestly presented as still incomplete. He refused, however, to back down under pressure: "We have, as our report to you demonstrates, been able to show that combinations of acidity and metals are capable of causing alterations in test systems that mimic what we find in nature and my article reported in layman's terms what we have found."

Recalling that the article "did *not* implicate any source" as the cause of the acid precipitation over New England, Vogelmann noted that the abrupt rise in aluminum concentrations after 1950 "is real. We, and most other groups, are aware that local sources play roles in the production and dissemination of acidic precipitations, but the evidence is that increasing stack height in smelting and refining, in pulp and paper and in power generation are factors in the wide geographical distribution of acidic materials, rather than the local fallout that existed prior to ca. 1950. . . . In this regard you have probably seen the recent draft report on the Environmental Protection Agency study which points up the long distance transport of sulphur dioxide and other pollutants."

Indeed, the EPA report, a thick, two-volume study titled *The Acidic Deposition Phenomenon and Its Effects*, had devoted nearly its entire 650-page first volume to the question of atmospheric emission, transport and deposition. The question of long-range transport of pollutants was also the subject of a pivotal 1983 National Academy of Sciences report, titled *Acid Deposition: Atmospheric Processes in Eastern North America*. The report concludes, in part: "If the emissions of sulphur dioxide from *all sources* in this region were reduced by the same fraction, the result would be a corresponding fractional reduction in deposition."

It was in the 1950s that utilities and other emission-producing industries began building the tall stacks that made long-range transport of pollutants possible. In the view of many researchers it was the added burden of pollutants arriving from distant points *plus* the output of local polluters that caused the measured upsurge in the acidity of New England and Eastern Canadian rain and snow—the same upsurge reflected in Vogelmann's tree core samples.

In the spring of 1983, AEP's original three-year grant to the Vermont project ran out, and Vogelmann was informed that it would not be renewed.

"They did it by a telephone call," he says. "And I've got to say this to their credit, they had agreed to fund us for three years and they did. They stuck with that. Two officials came last week and spent two days with us to review our work and there was a little stiffness in the air, but they came through with their part of the bargain. It's just that they weren't about to continue the funding. I think that they were a little bitter that they didn't get better publicity out of this.

"They feel that, 'gosh, we made a gesture and nobody recognized it and everybody's down on the power companies.' And they've got a point. But I told them, 'you guys have got real problems. Don't put your head in the sand here.'" (The fund cutoff will not halt the work at Camels Hump, since Vogelmann's team has found alternate sources of support.)

Of course, the utilities should not be faulted for trying to protect their own interests, by refusing to accept responsibility for emissions damages. As businessmen responsible to cost-conscious shareholders, their directors would find it difficult to do anything else. What is hard to understand, however, is the failure of industries that stand to lose heavily from the effects of acid deposition to likewise act in their own interests. Lumber companies, pulp and paper manufacturers and the entire construction industry face massive losses if the kind of destruction observed in the Black Forest and Bavaria and in the Adirondacks and the Green Mountains should spread to other tracts of timber.

University of Wyoming economist Dr. Thomas Crocker, in a 1982 paper on the economic effects of acid rain, estimated that American lumber companies were already absorbing a deficit of "nearly $600 million annually in lost timber production" due to a reduction in tree growth caused by acid rain. He based his estimates on a 1978 report by the Panel on Nitrates of the National Academy of Sciences and National Research Council, which concluded that annual forest growth in the United States at the time of the study was being retarded by a factor of 5 percent by the effects of acid deposition.

A similar study by the National Research Council of Canada in 1977 estimated that direct annual forest losses attributable to acid rain in Canada at that time were "between $1.2 and $2.8 million." What might be at stake if the picture should worsen was pointed out by the Canadian Parliamentary Sub-

Committee on Acid Rain in its 1981 report *Still Waters: The Chilling Reality of Acid Rain*: "In 1978, the Canadian wood industries and pulp and paper industries employed 197,000 workers, or 15 percent of total manufacturing employment. Total value of shipments amounted to $17.67 billion. It is thus clear that Canada's forest resources are the basis for a significant proportion of domestic economic activity. . . . The Canadian forests are such a valuable resource that their protection is vital. In the United States, where the forest sector is much less important to the total economy, acid rain is estimated to cause annual damage in the hundreds of millions of dollars. It is therefore apparent that the potential for damage to Canadian forests is very high since a large part of these forestry resources lie in the most sensitive areas of Ontario and Quebec."

If damage should spread, the losses may not be felt immediately. Researchers in Sweden, for example, found that between 1950 and 1965 the growth rates of pine and spruce in southern parts of the country whose soils were sensitive to acidity declined by 0.3 percent. Between 1965 and 1974, however, growth trends reversed and an actual increase was recorded. According to the Swedish Ministry of Agriculture publication *Acidification Today and Tomorrow*, the reason for the unexpected increase may have been the fertilizing effect of the nitrogen compounds in acid precipitation: "On the one hand, increments of hydrogen and sulphate ions have an acidifying effect on the soil. This in turn may restrain the activity of the soil organisms, and less nitrogen will be released from the organic material in the soil. On the other hand, the increased deposition of nitrogen compounds from the air makes up for the reduced turnover in the soil, and may even have a fertilizing and production-boosting effect. In conjunction with climatic changes, this very increase in nitrogen deposition may have been the cause of the increase in forest growth during the period 1965–74. . . . However, established stands on an average soil in southwestern Sweden with maximum nitrogen deposition will have reached saturation within a 50-year period. If the deposition of nitrogen continues to increase then, the forest will cease to react to it by showing an increase in growth. This has already happened in Germany."

In short, any beneficial effects of excess nitrogen may eventually level off and, since other vital soil nutrients have been leached away in the interim, likely will be followed by a second, more precipitous drop in growth. Attempts to offset these negative results by liming forested areas could prove prohibitively expensive and in many cases impossible. Coupled with the vast extent of land involved, and the consequently vast amount of lime needed to cover it, are the evident physical barriers to application. Aerial sprays might not penetrate the canopy, while tractors could not maneuver in thick bush.

Obviously, the cost to forest industries of ameliorating the damage caused by acid deposition could prove substantial. Yet, as Domtar's Dr. Tomlinson reluctantly admits, few North American companies seem aware of the vulnerability of their position:

"I'm afraid this thing has been rather badly ignored by most people within the industry," he says. "I see some signs of movement. The situation is changing, but it's not a dramatic change yet. I think it's gradually getting through to people that there are some serious problems in Germany and they're quite likely related to what we have here in North America.

"I've been in Germany six or seven times in the last three years, and the German forest industry is very much concerned. I get letters from the director of the German paper and pulp association, and other groups that are extremely concerned. [In North America] you have individuals within companies who are quite concerned, but you don't find it as a company policy."

Part of the problem, Tomlinson believes, is simply a lack of information, and he cites a typical example. "I've got a letter here from a senior vice-president of a major pulp company. He writes: 'It's difficult for people, even technical people, to develop an accurate perspective on the acid precipitation issue. I do not have the time to study detailed scientific material in the depth that it deserves. I badly need some reliable summaries.' "

Tomlinson's own published papers, interpreting the work of Ulrich and other forest scientists, have helped fill the information gap, and the Domtar scientist believes his industry will eventually see the danger and demand changes. "It's a question of time," he concludes.

But whether North America's forests can afford the luxury of letting more time pass is an open question.

Kneeling with his hands in the dirt where he has been digging soil samples, the head of the Quebec government scientific team investigating the *bois-francs* maple diebacks pauses in his work and looks up at the trunk of a massive dead maple.

His name is Clement Gravel. He is a careful, deliberate man and when he speaks he speaks slowly, weighing his words.

"This is the twenty-third dying sugar bush we've observed," he says. "Each one has its own personality. Some are on hillsides, others on flat land, some are grazed by cattle, some not. Some are overexploited and others well cared for. At this one, we've marked 56 trees. We'll study them for at least two years—insects, diseases, parasites, diameter, height. We'll see what develops.'"

He reaches out and touches the trunk of the tree with his

hand and then, unaware of Vogelmann's earlier words and the irony of the reference, muses:

"There are all kinds of causes for this, like with cancer. There are people who don't smoke, but they die of it just the same. We're searching. We're more or less in the dark. But when I see a beautiful maple like this, I look at it as if it was a human being, and I ask myself, why is it dead? I don't know.

"I'm asking."

Four

Field, Farm and the Monuments of Man

The soil that covers the surface of the earth is not inert but alive, an environment in itself, as teeming as the underbrush of a rain forest or the outcrops of a coral reef, filled with energy, with movement, with interconnections more complex than the strategies of a chessboard.

Scientists trying to understand the connections drill out vertical sections, layered cores called "soil profiles," to study. But no matter how many samples are taken or how close together each drill hole, no two profiles are exactly the same. They are as unique as fingerprints.

One should not speak of soil, but of soils.

Just as taxonomists classify plants and animals, soil scientists have elaborated a system to help them see the order in chaos. Soils are grouped by general pattern, like with like, according to their texture, structure, porosity, weight, moisture, chemical and biological properties and according to the color and thickness of each lettered soil profile layer, or "horizon." In the same way that students memorize the familiar kingdom, phylum, class, order, family, genus and species of biological classifications, observers of the land, graduates of agricultural colleges like Iowa, Michigan State or Alberta know the major soil categories: order, suborder, group, family, series and type.

The orders have strange, Slavic-sounding names: luvisolic, gleysolic, podsolic, brunisolic. But they are not foreign. They are as close as a heartbeat, as life itself. Everything terrestrial depends on them, the whole structure of forest, field and farm. In them, trees and crops find warmth, moisture, nourishment, an anchor for their roots against the wind. Destroy the soil and the edifice of life on dry land crumbles.

In a strictly literal sense, the potential effects of current levels of acid rain on agricultural soils are unknown. Experimentation is in its earliest stages and, with only a few exceptions, systematic field observations of crops in vulnerable regions have barely begun. But to conclude from this that no one has any inkling what acid deposition might do to soils and the plants that grow on them would be a mistake. The basic laws of chemistry, earlier studies of naturally acidic soils and the small but growing number of field and laboratory observations of actual pollution effects show that some of the impacts could be brutal.

Take, for example, the question of ion exchange. All plants need a continual input of at least 16 chemical elements to develop normally and complete their life cycles. Carbon, oxygen and hydrogen, which constitute 90 percent of plant weight, are absorbed from the atmosphere or from water, but the other 13 elements, which are classed as macro- or micronutrients according to the amounts found in plant tissues, are absorbed through ion exchange between roots and soil. Just as an upsurge in hydrogen and metal ions in a lake can upset the delicate osmoregulatory balance of fish, a similar influx in soils can derail the ionic exchange processes of plants. It is *only* in the ionic form of the elements, the state they achieve when dissolved in water or clinging to the surface of soil colloids, that the elements can be absorbed by plants.

Calcium, potassium and magnesium, all of them macronutrients, dissociate into cations, or positively charged ions, in water. They are absolutely necessary if a plant is to survive. Calcium is required by plants for cell-wall synthesis; as mentioned earlier, trees require it for lignification, the manufacture of wood tissue. Potassium, essential for growth, bolsters disease resistance in plants, strengthens the stalks of grains and aids the winter hardiness of perennial legumes. Magnesium is a key constituent of the all-important chlorophyll.

In unpolluted soils, compounds containing these elements are broken up by the action of naturally occurring carbonic and acetic acids and by decomposition bacteria. The elements thus liberated adhere to the surfaces of soil particles or are released directly into the soil solution (the liquid that fills the pores between particles of soil) in the form of ions. The ions in solution are available to plants immediately, while those held on particle surfaces are released gradually as their dissolved counterparts require replacement. The roots of plants "trade" or exchange these positive ions for surplus hydrogen ions already held in their own tissues.

Where the precipitation is acid, however, ever-increasing hydrogen ions burden the soil solution, along with a rising population of positive aluminum and other ions released from soil clays by the action of sulphuric and nitric acids. The hydrogen cations "bump," or exchange places with, the nutrient cations held on particle surfaces, releasing the latter into solution. An initial "zap" of nutrients sometimes occurs, prompting a sudden upsurge in plant growth. But soon the reserve of nutrients stored by the particles is exhausted, and any "bumped" cations not immediately absorbed by plants are washed away. Because aluminum is much more abundant than calcium, magnesium or potassium, considerable quantities of it remain after the other ions have gone. The result, for plants, is that the number of nutrient ions becomes proportionately less and less, and the roots are eventually reduced to exchanging hydrogen for hydrogen—or, worse, for toxic aluminum ions. A macronutrient shortage ensues, coupled with an increase in acidity as well as in the effects of toxic metals.

Anions, or negatively charged ions, are also affected by excess acidity. The micronutrients boron and molybdenum and the macronutrient phosphorus exist in soil solutions as negatively charged borates, molybdates and phosphates, which plant roots ordinarily take up by exchanging them for negative hydroxide and bicarbonate ions. As the plant tissues continue to become more acidic, however, there are proportionately fewer hydroxide ions available for trade, as well as fewer nutrient anions in the soil.

Phosphorus, which is most easily available to plants between pH 5.5 and pH 7, reacts with metals in acid soils to form insoluble compounds that roots cannot absorb. Without it, plants are deprived of an essential chemical aid in the transfer and storage of energy for biochemical reactions. Boron and molybdenum are needed only in trace amounts, but their absence can be disastrous. Molybdenum, for example, is needed to permit plants to utilize nitrates. Without sufficient molybdenum, cauliflower and broccoli develop "whip tail" disease, which twists and elongates leaves while killing the leaf tissue along its midrib.

Changes in pH can also affect soil "tilth" (the structure of soil grains or aggregates and their resistance to breakdown by rainfall and tillage), as well as the rate of decomposition of organic matter by bacteria; the growth of nitrogen-fixing bacteria; growth of disease-causing fungi; and the survival of animals, such as earthworms, that aerate the soil.

The germination and growth of seeds is dependent upon

tilth. Small seeds, such as grass, need a fine tilth, while large seeds like beans and corn find a coarser tilth more suitable. The ideal situation for most crops is a soil with aggregates ranging between one and five millimeters in diameter and extending from the surface down to the level of the underground water table.

Stable soil grains and pores permit rapid water intake and adequate drainage, while facilitating the contact between seeds and soil that allows moisture to reach the seeds and begin germination. If soil aggregates cannot maintain their structure, but disintegrate after wetting and drying, a hard surface crust may form, blocking the entry of both water and air.

Acidification of a soil can harm its structure in several ways. First, as Dr. Murray Miller of the Saskatchewan Institute of Pedology explains, calcium is "an integral component" of the chemical system that creates and maintains soil aggregates. Any child who has played with a pair of magnets knows that opposite electrical charges attract each other, while like charges repel. In the soil, certain clay particles carry a negative charge and would normally repel one another, except for the neutralizing effect of positively charged calcium cations which, when they adhere or "adsorb" onto a clay particle surface, balance out the repellent effect and allow the clays to cling together.

"Calcium will satisfy the negative charge on the clay and bind the particles," says Miller. "But of course acidification, by definition, implies the replacement of calcium ions by hydrogen and aluminum ions, which don't have the same effect. The structural stability of the soil is thus reduced as pH falls."

He cautions, however, that the calcium function is "not the major factor in soil structure" but only one of several components, and adds that "the organic matter content of the soil is more important." Numerous microscopic soil organisms, chiefly bacteria, secrete complex carbon compounds called mucillages, which also help cement aggregates together. At low pH their metabolism is slowed, and when soils become very acid many of them are destroyed.

Certain legumes, especially hay crops and sods, also secrete cementing agents. In addition, their roots help compress particles and dehydrate the soil, a necessary step in the formation of aggregates. The health of these crops—alfalfa, trefoil, clover—is dependent in part on their cooperative, or symbiotic, relationship with a group of bacteria called *Rhizobia* (*spp.*) that live in the nodules on the plant roots. These bacteria transform or "fix" free nitrogen into forms the plants can use, but their growth is inhibited when soils fall below pH 6. It is a domino effect; acidification reduces the population of *Rhizobia*, the lack of *Rhizobia* slows the development of legumes and as a result fewer cementing compounds are produced.

In short, excess acid, particularly in soils that are not regularly or adequately "amended" by treatment with lime, is unlikely to do much good for soil structure.

Rhizobia, of course, are not the only bacteria adversely affected by acidification. As noted earlier in connection with forest soils, the microbes that decompose organic matter, making the nutrient elements it contains available to crops, are also inhibited by a drop in pH. So is the growth of a group of related organisms called actinomycetes, which also aid in organic decomposition.

The nourishment of plants is thus hampered in three ways when pH levels fall: by the disruption of ion exchange through the roots, by the leaching of nutrient ions from the soil solution and also by the slowing of decomposition.

The effects of acidification create a vicious circle, which becomes more vicious as it revolves through the soil system. As the population of bacteria declines, various species of acid-tolerant fungi move in and occupy the vacant environmental niche. Among the latter are several disease-causing groups, such as *Pythium*, which causes stem rot, root rot and "damping off" in infested crops.

Although most fungi seem to tolerate acidity, one of the few groups that does not is formed of those that establish a so-called "mycorrhizal" relationship with the roots of various plants. In this relationship—which, like that of the nitrogen-fixing *Rhizobia* bacteria, is a mutually beneficial one—the root-like mycellium of the fungi form a filamentous sleeve or case around the roots of the host plant, or in some cases actually penetrate the root cells. Once in place, the mycorrhiza serves as a sort of living filter, drawing nutrients from the soil and transmitting them to the plant roots in a form more suited for their absorption.

Mycorrhizal fungi populations tend to decline as soils acidify.

Also thinned as the land becomes more acid are the ranks of those creatures so well known to backyard gardeners and small boys with fishing poles: the earthworms. As British zoologist J. E. Satchell explained in his 1955 paper "Some Aspects of Earthworm Ecology," most species of earthworm prefer neutral or very slightly alkaline soils.

Below pH 5.4 the common nightcrawler, *Lumbricus terrestris*, normally cannot survive, while pH 5.2 seems to be the lower limit for the fieldworm *Allolobophora caliginosa*. Below pH 7 the red worm, *Lumbricus rubellus*, and the brandling worm, *Eisenia foetida*, both find survival a problem. According to Satchell, worms enter a state called "diapause" in acid soils, in which both reproduction and the worms' soil-improving functions cease. Describing earthworm responses to low pH, University of Wisconsin garden writer Jerry Minnich notes that worms will attempt to flee strongly acid soils and, once forced onto the surface, "will refuse to follow their instinct to burrow and will die within 24 hours."

Earthworms, of course, are highly beneficial to most soils.

Their burrows help to aerate the ground, increasing the availability of oxygen to plants and microorganisms, and also provide conduits through which water drainage can occur. In feeding they pass large amounts of mineral and organic matter
through their bodies, thus assisting in the chemical breakdown
of soil compounds and the release of nutrients into the soil solution. Their manure, called "castings," is several times richer
in nutrients than the soil the worms ingest, and some species
are capable of producing their own weight in castings every 24
hours. The earthworm population of a single acre can pass as
much as 15 tons of dry earth through their bodies annually,
and their burrows can extend as far as six feet down into the
ground. Their ceaseless burrowing is a crucial aid in breaking
up "hard pans"—solid, impermeable layers of soil—formed
when the repeated passage of heavy farm vehicles over a field
compacts the soil below plow depth. Such hard layers hamper
drainage and root development.

The destruction of earthworms is almost synonymous with
the destruction of soil health.

The damage acidification can do to field crops is not restricted to the indirect route of attacking them through the soil
and soil organisms. Authors of both the U.S. Environmental
Protection Agency report *The Acidic Deposition Phenomenon
and Its Effects* and the Canadian National Research Council
review *Sulphur and Its Inorganic Derivatives in the Canadian
Environment* warn that atmospheric SO_2 and sulphuric acids
are capable of causing direct plant tissue injury.

"In flowering plants, sulphur dioxide is absorbed mainly
through the stomata [openings on the underside of leaves that
regulate the exchange of water and gases] of the foliage," write
the Canadian authors. "It dissolves in the surface fluid to form
sulphites. . . . If the plant's capacity to oxidize sulphites is exceeded, the latter build up to toxic levels. Two conditions have
been recognized: One of chronic injury, usually associated

with sublethal concentrations of ambient SO_2 over a prolonged period, and one of acute injury resulting from higher concentrations operating over shorter periods. Chronic injury is usually typified by a general chlorosis or bleaching and acute injury is signalled by a plasmolysis [loss of water] of the cells and a necrotic [local, killing] collapse of the tissues. . . . Affected areas initially appear water-soaked, but later take on the marked silvering or bronzing. On grasses and [similar] plants the necrotic areas appear as streaks extending backwards from the tip."

Comparative studies in 1956 and 1969 of the relative susceptibility of common agricultural crops to such damage, the authors continue, showed that at least 22 staple crops were sensitive. They included several varieties of wheat, turnip, sweet potato, squash, spinach, rye, rhubarb, radish, pumpkin, peas, oats, lettuce, endive, clover, carrots, buckwheat, brussels sprouts, broccoli, beets, beans, barley and alfalfa.

The Canadian review also notes that "for crops sold partly on appearance [ornamentals, Christmas trees, such market garden produce as lettuce] injury alone suffices to destroy marketability. For crops harvested and processed in various ways [cereals, root crops, fruit, forest trees], injury may be tolerated provided not more than five percent of the leaf tissue suffers; above this, loss in yield has been found to be proportional to the leaf area injured."

Speaking of wet, as opposed to gaseous, deposition, the EPA report states that, as experimental evidence with simulated acid rain shows, "a wide range of plant species is believed to be sensitive to direct injury from some elevated level of wet acidic deposition. . . . In addition to the physical abrasion of superficial [leaf] wax structure by raindrops, leaves exposed to rainfall of pH 3.2 appeared to weather more rapidly than did leaves of pH 5.6."

The report adds that "through the application of simulated

rainfall in controlled experiments, precipitation acidity has been studied as a variable influencing the leaching rate of various cations and organic carbon from foliage. Foliar losses of potassium, magnesium and calcium from bean and maple seedlings were found to increase as the acidity of simulated rain increased. Tissue injury occurred below pH 3, but significant increases in leaching rates occurred [at] as high as pH 4."

The U.S./Canadian Work Group on Transboundary Air Pollution, in its 1981 interim report, gathered the results of numerous simulated acid rain experiments, showing the effects— from foliar lesions to dehydration and death—of precipitation at different pH levels on 31 economically important tree and field crop species. Several studies cited, and others completed since the report's publication, have demonstrated a clear connection between the rain and direct plant damage. In a 1977 series of experiments conducted at the EPA's Corvallis, Oregon, research center, bush bean plants were treated once a week for six weeks with simulated acid mist at pH levels ranging from 5.5 to 2. Researchers reported that "leaf injury developed on plants exposed to acid concentrations below pH 3 and many leaves developed a flecking symptom similar to that caused by ozone. . . . Reductions in plant weight and chlorophyll content were detected across the pH gradient. Seed and pod growth was reduced at some intermediate acid depositions even though no visible foliar injury developed.

"Foliar losses of nitrogen, calcium, magnesium and phosphorus increased with decreases in acid mist pH, whereas foliar potassium concentrations were unaffected by acid mist treatment."

A set of experiments performed in 1981 and reported in the *New Phytologist* also demonstrated that simulated acid rain had a markedly adverse effect on the seed yields of soybeans, which is a staple of livestock feed and a major U.S. export crop. Scientists found that "seed yields of soybeans exposed twice weekly to simulated rain of pH 4.1, 3.3 and 2.7 were, respectively, 10.7, 16.8 and 22.9 percent *below* yields of plants exposed to simulated rain of pH 5.6. . . . In both experiments the observed decrease in seed yields was due to a decrease in number of pods per plant." Explaining that standard agronomic practices, *including* the application of lime to the soil medium in which the crops were grown, were followed, the scientists noted that "the economic implications of changes in soybean yeilds could be significant.

"For example, a one percent reduction in seed yields of soybeans grown in the northeastern United States (Delaware, Illinois, Indiana, Kentucky, Maryland, Michigan, New Jersey, New York, Ohio, Pennsylvania and Virginia) during 1980 would represent a loss of $53.4 million."

Acid precipitation in many parts of the states mentioned currently averages pH 4, with individual rainstorms registering at levels of pH 3.5 and below.

Two points of special importance are highlighted by these soybean experiments. First, as the National Clean Air Coalition states: "Soybeans . . . are the second most important cash crop in the U.S., valued at over $14 billion in 1979." Second, the sharp drop in seed yields took place *despite* the application of lime and fertilizers.

Supporters of industry claims that acid deposition cannot harm crops frequently cite the fact that most farm acreages are limed and treated with fertilizers as cause for complacency. Any adverse effects of acidification would be offset by these amendments, industry spokesmen claim.

Of course, to a certain extent, such claims are true. Liming does offset acidification, and the application of fertilizers can replace nutrients leached from the soil. It is even true, as some industry-financed scientists have emphasized, that an influx of the sulphur and nitrogen compounds in acid deposition can be beneficial toward crops growing in regions whose soils are naturally deficient in such elements. Nitrogen and sulphur—in moderate amounts—are as necessary to plant growth as carbon and oxygen.

One scientist employed by the Tennessee Valley Authority, which until recently was one of the worst polluters on the continent, went so far in a newspaper interview as to describe some crops as "addicted" to pollution. "If we clean up the air, then the cost of putting sulphur back into fertilizers should be considered," he said.

But other scientists are more realistic. Says the EPA's Dr. Norman Glass: "The notion that it is essential or desirable, or even marginally acceptable to continue supplying sulphur indiscriminately by using polluted masses of air instead of controlled applications of fertilizer is just that—fertilizer."

Confidence in the miracle-working attributes of lime is revealed as even more misplaced when it is recalled that both lime and fertilizers cost money—cash that the farmer must come up with out of his own pocket. Agricultural lime currently sells at between $7 and $10 per metric tonne, and the usual rate of application in a mixed farming situation in North America is around two tonnes per acre.

As Swedish Ministry of Agriculture scientists reported in their 1982 publication *Acidification Today and Tomorrow,* "At the present time our plowland is being acidified a good deal faster than our forestland. The important causes are extra loads such as fertilization with ammonium-bearing fertilizers, extraction of ever larger harvests and [atmospheric] deposition of acidifying substances. . . . Overall calculations indicate an average lime demand of 120 to 200 kilograms per hectare per year. . . . Out of the 200 kg of lime needed per hectare, 10 to 30 kg is needed to keep acid deposition in check."

An annual application of "about 600,000 tonnes of lime" is needed to compensate in full for the current overall plowland acidification, the Swedes note. The addition of chemical fertilizers to replace the potassium, calcium and other nutrients leached away as soil pH falls is no less expensive. Whipsawed for the past two decades by the constantly inflating costs of fuel and machinery and the effects of crop price returns that fail to keep pace, farmers can ill afford even the moderate rise in individual overheads that present levels of acidity may cause. Future increases in the land's acid burden could put some marginal enterprises in serious danger.

Financial losses on field crops injured by acid rain and the price of soil amendments to offset the rain's effects are not the only problems acid deposition poses for farmers. As the Ontario Ministry of Agriculture and Food publication *Ontario Soils* warns: "Soil pH is important in determining the availability of heavy metals, including lead, mercury and cadmium. In general, the pH should exceed 6.5 in order to minimize potential toxicity problems."

Both pastured livestock, which may graze on plants contaminated by toxic metals or drink contaminated water, and human beings, who will eventually eat the livestock, could be exposed to health risks due to the mobilization of metals by acid rain. The metal component in soils and farm water supplies can be increased by either direct deposition from stack gases or by the release of previously bound metals from soil compounds through the chemical action of acids in the soil solution.

The metal content of stack gases is highest, of course, in the smoke from smelters, whose purpose for existence is to extract metals such as copper, iron and zinc from their ores. Extraordinarily high volumes of such metals have been found in the soils, plants and waters near such installations as the Inco smelter at Sudbury. However, the metals fraction in electric power plant plumes is also high. For example, coal, oil and natural gas, the most common power plant fuels, all contain small amounts of mercury, which is released by combustion. The weighted average of the mercury concentrations in coals is usually in the area of 0.3 to 0.35 parts per million. Studies in 1971 and 1977 of the mercury vapor concentrations in the stack gas of large coal-fired power generating stations in Ontario, Canada, found amounts ranging from 40 to 80 micrograms per cubic meter. The average was 43 micrograms per cubic meter.

As the authors of the Canadian National Research Council report *Effects of Mercury in the Canadian Environment* explain, mercury vapor may be transported long distances via the same atmospheric mechanisms that transport SO_2. "Atmospheric transport clearly seems to be the dominant process for long-range movements [of mercury]," the report says. "The principal reason for suggesting that mercury is transported great distances by air is the observation that mercury is present above background levels in such remote areas as the Greenland and Antarctica ice caps. . . . It is widely supposed that the atmosphere is essentially cleaned of its mercury content by even mild precipitation."

Interestingly, the report notes, "the first Greenland ice studies seemed to indicate that from the earliest recorded observation to the mid-twentieth century the amount of mercury in precipitation remained more or less constant, and *since then it has apparently doubled* [author's emphasis]." In other words, since 1950, the pattern of mercury concentrations has followed the same sequence as that of the acidity of rainfall and the aluminum content in tree rings observed by Vermont's Dr. Vogelmann.

Mercury is one of the most biotoxic elements known. Particularly in its methylated form (methyl mercury), it is capable of severely damaging the nervous systems of animals and of causing serious birth defects in their young. Some of the toxic effects it can produce include ataxia (unsteadiness), abnormalities in gait and reflexes, lethargy, loss of sensation in tissues, mental retardation, impaired vision and speech, spontaneous abortion and general disruption of body functions. "Generally," note the authors of the Canadian mercury report, "the neurological signs of methyl mercury toxicity are not reversible."

In addition to being irreversible, mercury tends to become more concentrated as it is passed on up the food chain from one species to another, accumulating in especially large amounts in certain aquatic carnivores. Although the average level of mercury in most foods is generally around 0.02 parts per million, recent studies of fish and wildlife consumed by native peoples in the far north found levels as high as 37.2 ppm in seal livers eaten by Eskimos, 12.1 ppm in the breast muscles of common mergansers and 15.7 ppm in the lateral muscle of northern pike eaten by Ontario Indians.

As the Canadian report also notes, "cultivated soils generally contain more mercury than do uncultivated soils because mercury compounds have been used as fungicides and pesticides." Terrestrial plants may actually suffer injury from mercury compounds while concentrating it in their tissues. Sugar beets grown in an enclosed space showed leaf damage after only five hours' exposure to 0.28 milligrams of mercury vapor per cubic meter of air; and mercurial solutions used as seed treatments have been known to reduce seed viability if the mercury concentration is too high.

Of course, it does not follow from these facts that elevated levels of mercury are building up in domestic livestock, especially in livestock raised on grain in feedlots rather than pastured. Nor does it mean that there is any immediate danger to human consumers of farm products. Indeed, recent samplings show that the mercury content in most foods consumed by North Americans is two and a half times *less* than the maximum level recommended by the U.N. Food and Agriculture Organization and World Health Organization.

Although terrestrial plants, including agricultural crops, do take up mercury from both the soil and the atmosphere, they tend to do so in smaller amounts than do aquatic organisms. Tracer-aided studies conducted in 1975 showed that there is an apparent barrier in some plants preventing the translocation of mercury compounds from roots to plant tops above ground, where animals would eat them. The mercury report's authors add that "of the various meats that man is accustomed to consuming, only those from aquatic environments are derived from carnivorous creatures; otherwise it is almost always herbivores which are consumed. Therefore, the terrestrial food chain leading to the human being has one and often two less trophic levels than the aquatic food chain." That is to say, the terrestrial chain has one or two less chances to concentrate mercury before it reaches human palates.

Mercury is thus unlikely to be present—yet—in livestock in high enough volumes to cause symptoms of toxicity, or to pose any short-term danger to humans. But it has entered the food chain, it has been increasing since the 1950s and its effects are known to be cumulative. In the long run, it is not apt to do either men or animals any good.

And mercury is only one of many metals whose presence is being magnified as the environment continues to acidify. As noted earlier in discussing forests, aluminum is easily mobilized from acid soils—a fact that takes on considerable importance when it is realized that aluminum is one of the most abundant metals on this planet. Compounds of aluminum by themselves make up more than 15 percent of the earth's surface and form the major clay component of most soils. In acid soils in the United States, clays are primarily aluminosilicates. Ordinarily, the aluminum in these clays is bound harmlessly, unavailable to the soil solution in which measurable amounts of soluble aluminum are found only below pH 5.5. Once the pH begins to fall, however, the release of aluminum may, depending on which mineral it is bound to, be surprisingly rapid. One of the most plentiful clay aluminosilicates, kaolinite, breaks down fairly quickly as pH decreases, producing water, silicon hydroxides and free aluminum ions.

Aluminum is known to be toxic to plants. As the authors of the EPA's review of acid deposition note, a 1981 study showed that "aluminum toxicity is believed to be a primary factor in limiting plant root development (depth and branching) in many acidic subsoils of the southeastern United States." Legumes such as alfalfa (the major component in hay crops and forage rations fed to cattle) are also known to be highly sensitive to aluminum poisoning.

Relatively little research has been done on the possible direct toxic effects of aluminum on domestic animals, but significant traces of the metal have been detected in cows' milk. According to Thomas D. Luckey, in *Metal Toxicity in Mammals*, common symptoms of aluminum poisoning include "skin lesions, nervous afflictions, gastrointestinal disturbance, growth retardation, and fibrous peritonitis." Laboratory experiments using cats also have shown disturbing effects. In a series of studies in the early 1970s, aluminum hydroxide (the most toxic form of the metal) was applied to the cerebral tissues of cats, which subsequently developed symptoms of neurological degeneration resembling those of senility in humans.

As Luckey has pointed out, excessive doses of any metal, even the iron animals need to keep their blood healthy, can cause adverse effects, and the EPA report agrees. "Any metal can be toxic if soluble in sufficient quantities," its authors state. "However, a decrease in soil pH can create metal toxicity problems for vegetation. Zinc, copper and nickel toxicities have occurred frequently in a variety of acid soils. Iron toxicity occurs only under flooded conditions. . . . Toxicities of lead, cobalt, beryllium, arsenic and cadmium occur only under very unusual conditions. . . . Aluminum and manganese toxicities are the most prominent growth-limiting factors in many, if not most, acidic soils."

A 1966 study of factors affecting the growth of the symbiotic relationship between beans and *Rhizobia* bacteria in acid soils found that the addition of 40 ppm of manganese reduced nitrogen fixation efficiency or the numbers of nodules on the plant roots. In animals, excessive amounts of manganese can cause nephritis, cirrhosis of the liver, anorexia and muscular fatigue. According to Luckey, "massive feeding of [ionic] manganese to experimental animals retards growth, and causes calcium loss and poor absorption of iron, which leads to anemia, negative phosphorus balance and rickets."

Cadmium is readily absorbed by plant roots and, unlike mercury, translocated to plant tops where grazing livestock may ingest it. Mammals accumulate cadmium, which can replace zinc in some of their enzyme systems. Elevated levels of cadmium in both animals and humans have been related to the incidence of hypertension and cardiovascular disease. According to Luckey, cadmium in excessive amounts is "toxic to all tissues. Symptoms include growth retardation, impaired kidney function, poor reproductive capacity, hypertension, tumor formation and poor lactation [milk production]."

Other, unexpected results may occur as the land and the vegetation on it acidify. It is possible, for example, that a sufficiently drastic drop in pH could affect soil temperature, because low pH curtails the growth of the decomposition bacteria that break down organic litter on the soil surface. According to *Ontario Soils*, "The temperature of a soil with depth depends on the thermal conductivity of the soil materials; soil minerals are good conductors while organic matter is relatively poor. . . . Coarse-textured soils such as a sandy loam warm up in the spring at a faster rate than a fine-textured clay." The continual buildup of a thick layer of undecomposed organic debris could thus become an eventual factor in deciding the length of the growing season.

Another factor of far greater potential importance is the possible synergistic effect of several pollutants acting in concert. For example, ozone (O_3) has been identified as a serious threat to agricultural crops. Produced through the photochemical reactions of hydrocarbons and nitrogen oxides in the atmosphere, it has particularly harsh effects on both soybeans and wheat. According to the National Clean Air Coalition, "The National Crop Loss Assessment Program found that ozone pollution results in yield losses of $1.9 to $4.5 billion a year for corn, wheat, soybeans and peanuts. These figures, based on 1978 data, show a loss of about five percent of the total U.S. agricultural production."

The U.S./Canada Work Group on Transboundary Air Pollution warns: "Recent evidence suggests that generalizations concerning effects on crops from experiments with O_3 alone, or with acid precipitation alone, may underestimate the interactive effects of exposures to these two pollutants. Further research is needed to determine if acid precipitation enhances the likelihood of actual yield reductions in areas also experiencing repeated exposures to elevated concentrations of O_3."

It should be evident, reviewing what scientists already know, that the multitude of effects produced in soils and crops by the millions upon millions of hydrogen ions that are the end result of acid rain are, to say the least, cause for uneasiness. The final dénouement of the processes they are setting in motion now could someday strike, quite literally, at the roots of the human species' food supply.

But the destructive impact of acid deposition on the works of mankind is not limited to agriculture. Also attacked are our shelters, our tools and—what perhaps sets us apart from other species—our cultural expression in works of art. Metal, mortar, paper or stone, everything shaped by human hands is threatened: "Two years ago I constructed this part of my house," says Dorset, Ontario, trapper John McLennan, gesturing around his living room. "If we left our saws or our planes out where the first drops of rain hit on a wet day, we could *see* the rust form right in the drop on that tool. We could see it happen right under our eyes. Now maybe that was going on twenty years ago, but I don't remember it. I'm sure there was a time when we could be a little more careless.

"I have a little .410 gauge shotgun that I've had most of my life, and I've got rust on the barrel. My young lads just used it a time or two, and the last time forgot to wipe it off, and right away it had rust. I've had that gun a long time and I haven't seen rust form that fast before. I'm sure we didn't see that kind of thing years ago."

McLennan is probably right. The level of acidity of Ontario's "ground zero" area rains weren't as high two decades ago as they are today, and it is a thoroughly documented fact that sulphur pollution rapidly increases the corrosion process in metals. Numerous experiments and field trials with metal samples have documented the fact repeatedly since the 1930s.

In Sweden, for example, a series of comparisons of metal samples exposed to the atmosphere between 1958 and 1970 at various urban and rural locations showed that carbon steel corroded at a rate of eight micrometers per year in relatively unpolluted rural locations, but that the same steel corroded at a rate of 30 micrometers per year—nearly four times faster—in a sulphur-polluted urban environment. Copper samples in the same tests corroded at a rate of 0.6 micrometers a year in the rural locations, but at one full micrometer per year in the urban area. The service life of nickel-plated steel in the rural areas was rated at 3.5 years but was reduced to only 1.9 years in the urban sample locations.

As the authors of *Acidification Today and Tomorrow* state:

> A dose-effect relationship has been established for certain metals that are important in the technical context. In the case

of carbon steel and zinc, among other metals, these relationships can be turned to account for such purposes as classifying the corrosivity of the atmosphere. . . . An investigation of the corrosion rate [of unprotected carbon steel] in six American cities shows that *the mean annual sulphur dioxide concentration is a measure of the corrosivity of the air.*

The corrosion rates of copper are decidedly lower in a rural atmosphere (below one micrometer per year) than in an urban atmosphere (one to two micrometers per year) or an industrial atmosphere (two to five micrometers per year).

The corrosion rate of nickel plate is 1.8 micrometers per year in Newark—with an urban/industrial atmosphere—and six micrometers per year in the heavily polluted air of Birmingham. These figures are to be compared with the low rate of 0.25 micrometers per year found in rural atmospheres.

The U.S. Environmental Protection Agency, in its report on acid deposition, states that "the rusting of metals is an oxidation process that is accelerated by the presence of acidic pollutants. . . . in the presence of SO_2 and moisture, iron corrosion proceeds from randomly distributed centers associated with the deposition of particulate matter."

Noting that in many cases laboratory experiments have been unable to duplicate field situations closely enough to be valid, the EPA authors add that "the set of laboratory experiments most clearly approximating field conditions was conducted by F. H. Haynie in 1976. Various materials were exposed to controlled pollutant concentrations and moisture conditions at levels encompassing those found in ambient urban atmospheres. Sunlight and the formation of dew were also simulated. . . . The results showed *a strong, statistically significant relationship between steel corrosion and SO_2 concentration, together with high humidity.*"

In 1979, the International Joint Commission reported that as much as 50 percent of the corrosion damage to North American automobiles could be caused by the effects of sulphur pol-

lution, including acid rain. But ordinary motorists aren't the
only vehicle owners likely to suffer. According to Michigan
State University's Professor Robert Summitt, an engineering
consultant to the U.S. Air Force, acid rain is one of the major
causes of corrosion attacking the nation's fleet of B-52
bombers.

In some cases, Summitt told reporters in a 1983 interview,
corrosion is so bad "you can pop the rivets right out of the
wings with your fingers." Two metal alloys employed frequently in military aircraft are aluminum/copper and alumi-
num/magnesium/zinc. Both alloys "corrode like crazy," Summitt says, adding that "civilian planes are built with lower-
stress alloys. They don't corrode as much." Echoes Lt. Col.
Garth Cooke of Wright-Patterson Air Force Base: "Most of our
older weapons systems, like the B-52s, have corrosion problems that are costing a great deal of money. Pollution is a major
accelerator of the corrosion process."

The Air Force must spend more than $1 billion per year to
handle its corrosion problems.

More peaceful national symbols are also being affected. In
1982, National Park Service engineers reported that the
Statue of Liberty in New York Harbor has been seriously corroded. The salt air of the Atlantic Ocean, ambient SO_2 in the
New York atmosphere and acid rain have combined to wreak
havoc on the steel and copper monument that has symbolized
America since 1886. The iron bars that support the statue's
copper skin have in some cases been eaten away to half their
original thickness, and the copper skin itself has also been considerably thinned. Millions of dollars will be needed to repair
the destruction.

Also ravaged as the acidity of our atmosphere increases year
by year are buildings, bridges, statues and monuments made
of brick and mortar or of stone—especially limestone, sand-

stone and marble. The destructive chemical reactions involved take many forms, depending in part on the material being attacked and in part on whether the sulphuric compounds involved are in the gaseous, wet or dry particulate state. For example, gaseous SO_2 will react with stones composed of calcium carbonate ($CaCO_3$), such as limestone or marble, or with stones whose cementing agents include substantial amounts of calcium carbonate. The primary reaction produces carbon dioxide and calcium sulphite. The calcium sulphite then oxidizes to become $CaSO_4$—common gypsum—which appears as a white crystalline or fibrous mass on the stone surface and is washed away by the rain. In time, the entire building or statue will be washed away. Gypsum makes an excellent insulating material, which is its main commercial use, but it isn't much good at resisting weather.

The process is only slightly different where wet deposition is involved; sulphuric acid (H_2SO_4) reacts with calcium carbonate to produce water, carbon dioxide and, once again, gypsum. Dry deposition involving various sulphates, such as ammonium sulphate, also produces gypsum. In sandstone, which is highly porous, gypsum crystals forming inside the pores can swell until the stress they create cracks the stone around them. Gypsum in solution can also migrate over the stone surface, trickling into nooks and crannies where the raindrops themselves cannot make contact.

Scientists have also begun investigating the possibility that certain bacteria living on the surface of limestone and sandstone structures may play a part in destroying their own homesites. The "Bug that Ate Minneapolis" in grade B horror films could turn out in reality to be an army of microbes, and not even giant ones at that. Researchers hypothesize that certain species of bacteria metabolize atmospheric sulphur dioxide, which they convert to sulphuric acid in order to use the acid as a digestive fluid. The acid in turn attacks the calcium carbonate in the stone, liberating both gypsum and carbon dioxide, which serves as the bacterial nutrient.

If this hypothesis is correct, billions of microbes stimulated by polluted air may quite literally be eating our cities away.

The results of these chemical and possibly biological activities have already become shockingly obvious in cities throughout the northern hemisphere. A classic example is the widely reprinted pair of photographs of an ornamental statue at Herten Castle in the outskirts of the heavily polluted Ruhr region of West Germany. The figure, carved in 1702, had sustained only very moderate damage up to 1908, when the first of the pair of photographs was taken. When the second photo was taken in 1969, however, the transformation was startling. What had been a graceful female figure in flowing robes in 1908 had in 60 years been reduced to an almost shapeless blob, devoid of features. The creative vision of the sculptor who had laboriously carved the figure nearly three centuries ago had been turned to gypsum and washed away, like a castle in the sand.

In Greece, where the marble of the Acropolis is dissolving, in London, where Saint Paul's Cathedral is being eroded, in Washington, D.C., where the white Lee marble of the Capitol is pitted with craters a quarter inch or more in diameter, the situation is the same. Some of the finest art and architecture in the world is being destroyed by the acid in the air.

A host of other materials, from leather and paint to textiles, are also under assault. According to the EPA's 1983 study of acid deposition, acidic gases corrode electrical contacts, degrade the film base of photographic negatives and weaken the tensile strength of cotton and nylon. "In field tests in St. Louis, cotton duck exposed to varying SO_2 levels showed a direct relationship between loss in tensile strength and increasing SO_2 concentration," the EPA reports. "Nylon fabrics . . . lost 80 percent of their strength in the presence of SO_2." Sulphur pollutants also degrade paper and produce "statistically significant erosion rate increases" in paints exposed to the air, particularly oil-based house paints.

So pervasive are the all-destroying sulphur and nitrogen compounds in the air that numerous museums, including the Library of Congress in Washington, D.C., and Chicago's Newbury Library, have been forced to install small-scale atmospheric "scrubbers" to filter pollutants from incoming air and protect their unique collections. Microfilmed records of historic documents and archives are especially vulnerable.

The cost of this material destruction and of the defensive measures required to prevent or repair it has not yet been accurately calculated, and given the priceless nature of some of the objects being corroded, such a task may be impossible. Various educated guesses have been made, nearly every one of them sobering.

In 1978, the U.S. President's Council on Environmental Quality estimated that property damage due to acid rain amounted to more than $2 billion per year, while the National Research Council of Canada in 1977 estimated the damage inflicted by sulphur emissions upon buildings alone at $285 million annually. Such estimates, however, must inevitably fall short of describing the true value of what is being lost. Although its message was muted by the dry language of academia, the U.S./Canada Work Group on Transboundary Air Pollution put its finger on the real problem in 1981, when it stated: "The patina of history cannot be replicated. The sources of supply for historic building materials are limited, if not extinct. Quarries have been exhausted, and stands of first growth timber are scarce. The pool of skilled craftsmen and artisans, able to extract and shape these materials, is diminishing. As in the case of many sensitive ecological systems which are being altered, degradation of certain man-made structures is an irreversible process. . . . measures of the net loss by deterioration must embrace aesthetic and historical contributions, and not rely on monetary scales alone."

In simpler terms, the artifacts of our history as a people, and the history of our neighbors, are irreplaceable. Once ruined, washed away in a puddle of dissolved gypsum, they are gone for good.

And so is a part of our national soul.

Five

The Absence
of Well-Being

"It feels terrible.

"You start to wheeze when you inhale and sometimes when you exhale. It builds up and your airways start to close and it's harder to breathe. You can't breathe. You get short, little breaths—enough to live, but not as much as you want. Your chest feels stuffed and then, after about an hour, it will start to hurt. You get a big pain in your chest.

"The wheezing comes from up here in your throat, and your chest will swell, sort of, because your airways are closing up. And you keep getting pains, chest pains. You can't concentrate on what you're doing. You can only concentrate on your breathing.

"It's miserable."

Ed is 14, strong, a good athlete who spends a lot of time outdoors. But his youth and skill are not enough to overcome chronic bronchial asthma, a condition that has plagued him all of his life. Pollen, dust or aerosols can provoke it without warning, entering his mouth and nose with the air, flowing along the myriad passageways of the respiratory system, prompting a muscular reflex that chokes as brutally as a noose.

He is accustomed to it now, knowing from experience what to expect and in what order. The fright, the panic he felt years ago as a toddler, when his breath was first cut off, have been replaced by a weary familiarity with discomfort. Medication helps.

But there are times, even now, when the old fright comes back. After 14 years of dealing with it, the choking feeling still retains a certain sinister power, the power to terrify. This summer, on a family trip to Washington, D.C., it reasserted itself:

"It was the worst attack I've had," Ed says. "There wasn't as much wheezing beforehand, but I thought I was going to die. I just started to wheeze and it kept getting worse. I had chest pains. My throat was swelling and closing up. I couldn't breathe much. It felt like my breathing would stop altogether.

"Afterwards, when the attack was over, I still had chest pains for a week.

"I had a dream once that I was being dropped into the water by a bunch of Mafia guys, with my feet in cement, you know? And I was in the water, choking.

"Whew! I wouldn't want to die that way."

The mechanism that causes these attacks is thoroughly vicious, working as if it was deliberately designed to turn each part of the respiratory system against itself. In this, no part of the system seems to be overlooked, and air pollution, particularly sulphur in its variety of forms, accentuates each step, making it worse—making it bad enough, in fact, that people can die. And they do.

The system by which we breathe could be compared to the network of underground tunnels in a mine. The main entry shaft is the trachea, or "windpipe," in the throat, down which air from the nose passes en route to the lungs. This tunnel branches into two secondary routes, the right and left bronchi, which each in turn divide into at least 20 smaller units. Each of the latter also branches, and the branches branch, dividing and subdividing into smaller and smaller openings. The smallest, called bronchioles, terminate in more than three million tiny air sacs, or alveoli, bunched like clusters of delicate flowers in the lung. It is across the cell membranes of the alveoli that oxygen diffuses into the bloodstream and unneeded carbon dioxide passes out of the blood, to be expelled as waste into the outside air on exhalation.

Larger particles of dust and pollutants, those greater than five micrometers in diameter, are relatively harmless to the system, especially if they are inhaled through the nose. The hairs and mucous of the nasal cavity trap them and filter them out. Gaseous pollutants such as sulphur dioxide are also removed in passing through the nasal area. More than 95 percent of any SO_2 inhaled through the nose is absorbed by the mucous membranes of the nose and trachea, which convert the gas to sulphates.

Smaller particles, ranging from 0.5 to 5 micrometers, can escape this initial filtering effect, as do pollutants inhaled through the mouth, where protective hairs and mucous are absent. People engaged in strenuous activity—runners or snowshoers, a farmhand hefting 80-pound bales onto a hay wagon on a hot summer day, a boy playing hockey—tend to breathe through their mouths, and to breathe faster. Indeed, the harder a person works the less effective are the body's nasal filters. Particles in the medium-size range can thus be taken in and may penetrate as far as the bronchioles.

In most cases the particles are removed from the bronchioles after a few hours' residence by the action of the cilia: thin, hairlike growths that line the walls of the bronchi and bronchioles and oscillate in a continual wavelike motion. The cilia gradually move any foreign bodies up into the pharynx area, where they can be either swallowed or expectorated.

Only the smallest particles, those less than 1 micrometer in diameter, are able to avoid all of the system's defenses and penetrate as far as the alveoli themselves. There, with no cilia to sweep them out, they may remain for weeks or even months.

Unfortunately for asthmatics and those suffering from other respiratory disorders, an irritant need not actually reach the alveoli to prompt a reaction. Particles able to penetrate that far, including droplets of sulphuric acid that are less than 1 micrometer in size, are often among the most toxic pollutants, and the results they cause may be more damaging than those of gaseous SO_2. But once any irritant reaches beyond the trachea, it may trigger the reflex that brings on an attack.

When that happens, the smooth muscles that encircle the bronchi and bronchioles like tape wrapped around the handle of a baseball bat begin to contract, squeezing shut the openings through which air normally flows. The wheezing sound is the sound of air literally whistling, as it would between pursed lips, in its passage through the narrowing tunnels. Less oxygen enters the lungs and, because the muscles are constricted when the victim exhales as well, less waste air and carbon dioxide are expelled. The alveoli distend like millions of miniscule balloons filled with too much air, creating the full feeling in the chest, the sensation of swelling.

They are not distended with useful oxygen. Any oxygen that does manage to gain entry is quickly transmitted to the blood, where it is urgently needed. They are distended, instead, with useless stale air, constantly increasing. Often, as well, mucous is secreted in the lungs, forming sticky plugs that further block the already shrunken bronchioles.

What happens next depends on the type of asthma with which the victim is afflicted, the severity of the attack or the toxicity of the foreign particles that induced it. If medication is used, the crisis may simply wear off and breathing return to normal. If the victim is unlucky, however, the symptoms may worsen. A wracking cough may appear, along with vomiting.

If the condition persists or the victim is weakened by age, infection or other complications, an intractable situation may develop, lasting a week or even longer. Breathing becomes labored. The lack of oxygen and excess of carbon dioxide cause lips and fingernails to become bluish. The cough becomes hacking, and fever, often as high as 103° F, may appear. An elderly person, or someone afflicted with emphysema, heart problems or even a bad case of flu, may become exhausted to the point of sinking into a coma, or suffer cardiac arrest and die.

Any asthma attack causes suffering, and serious attacks mean enough torture for millions of people each day to warrant every effort at prevention. But the prospect of even one innocent person having to pay the ultimate price—being slowly choked, strangled gradually for days or weeks before dying—should be sufficient to give anyone pause. It is a truly ugly way to die, as bad as death by cancer.

Yet every year, according to the United States Congress' Office of Technology Assessment, the lives of an estimated 51,000 Americans and Canadians end in exactly that way, prematurely and needlessly, as a direct result of atmospheric sulphur pollution.

In a July 1982 report, OTA researchers working at Brookhaven National Laboratory estimated that "about two percent of the deaths per year in the U.S. and Canada might be attributable to atmospheric sulphur particulate pollution." An estimate of fatalities, of course, only covers a part of the picture. As the report added: "It has been estimated that, for every person dying from sulphate exposure, five persons are ill with lung disease, heart disease aggravated by lung dysfunctions, and respiratory infections aggravated by lung irritations."

The OTA report did not attempt to estimate the number of needless deaths attributable to pollution by nitrogen oxides, noting that "not enough is yet known" about the effects of NO_x. Nor did it attempt to quantify fatalities that could result from the indirect effects of acid precipitation, such as the consequences of increased amounts of toxic metals in the environment. The body count of 51,000 is consequently an underestimate.

Also a likely underestimate was a 1979 report by Robert Mendelsohn of the University of Washington and Guy Orcutt of Yale University, who blamed sulphates in the atmosphere for approximately 187,686 deaths per year in the United States.

Whatever the numbers, the evidence that sulphur in both its gaseous and liquid acid forms can cause serious respiratory problems is impossible to dismiss. So are the indications that nitrogen oxides are dangerous to health. Both epidemiology— statistical analysis of the occurrence of disease in actual populations—and experimental work under controlled laboratory conditions lead to the same conclusions.

Scientific work indicating the adverse health effects of gaseous SO_2 has been going on continually for decades, and an impressive body of evidence has been amassed. Spectacular events, such as the 1952 "killer fog" in London, England, whose combination of SO_2, sulphates and smoke proved fatal to 4,000 people, are well known, as are numerous occupational health studies showing the consequences of on-the-job exposure to SO_2. For example, the 1976 Ontario *Report of the Royal Commission on the Health and Safety of Workers in Mines*, stated that one in every 4.4 workers in the Inco converter plant at Copper Cliff had chronic bronchitis, as opposed to only one in 12 persons in control populations. The report cited SO_2 as the culprit.

As Stephen Stoker and Spencer Seager note in their text *Environmental Chemistry: Air and Water Pollution*: "Long-term effects resulting from extended exposure to low levels of SO_2 are known. Studies carried out under the Community Health and Environmental Surveillance System program of the U.S. Environmental Protection Agency show a definite correlation between the incidence of respiratory infection in children and the level of SO_2 pollution in the environment. The frequency of infection and diminished lung function increased with an increased residence time of a child in a polluted area."

The EPA studies also indicated that acute aggravation of asthma and other respiratory symptoms in elderly persons were associated with 24-hour exposure to SO_2 levels of 200 to 300 micrograms per cubic meter of air, while chronic effects were observed at 200 to 400 micrograms per cubic meter.

The American Lung Association, in its 1983 review *Sulphur Oxides and Public Health, Evidence of Greater Risks*, warned:

> Sulphur dioxide is toxic. In laboratory tests, exposure to the gas for less than one hour at concentrations of 0.25 to 0.5 parts per million was found to constrict the respiratory airways of asthmatics and also to cause wheezing and shortness of breath. Normal subjects have also shown respiratory symptoms when exposed to sulphur dioxide, but at higher concentrations.
>
> Studies have shown that SO_2 affects various physiological functions, including sensory processes, perceptions of irritation or pain and respiratory function. In healthy subjects at rest, respiratory and cardiovascular responses have been consistently observed at exposure levels of five parts per million. . . . Systematic study of the effects of SO_2 on asthmatics was initiated in 1980, when researchers observed bronchoconstriction, sometimes with wheezing and shortness of breath, at concentrations less than one part per million. . . . An increased incidence of colds has been noted within one week of exposure to one, five and 25 parts per million SO_2. . . . In other work, recovery from mild upper respiratory infections was impeded in subjects exposed to five parts per million SO_2 for several days.

The American Thoracic Society also had harsh words for SO_2 in a 1978 review of health-related studies:

From epidemiologic studies of populations exposed to sulphur oxides and particulates, *there is no question that increased ambient concentrations have been consistently associated in large cities with increased mortality* during episodes of air pollution [author's emphasis].

On days of high pollutant concentrations, aggravation of symptoms in subjects with pre-existing heart and lung disease occurs. In more polluted cities there is evidence for a greater prevalence of chronic respiratory disease in adults, an increased incidence of acute respiratory disease and depressed lung function in children and increased illness episodes and illness related absences in adults.

In short, where human health is concerned it is impossible to claim that SO_2, even in low concentrations, is harmless.

The malignant effects of sulphates, especially sulphuric acid, are less well documented, but the evidence is mounting. As Stoker and Seager note in *Environmental Chemistry*: "Sulphate aerosols are three to four times more powerful as irritants than SO_2. These small particles penetrate to the lungs where they become embedded. If the sulphur is not already in sulphate form, the moist lung environment provides appropriate oxidation conditions. *Sulphates are believed by many to be the most serious air-pollution health hazard* [author's emphasis]."

Experiments with laboratory animals as long ago as 1969 provided early evidence of this fact. The bronchoconstrictive potency of SO_2, sulphuric acid and several aerosols of sulphate salt were compared in one study, and H_2SO_4 was found to "induce a greater bronchoconstrictive effect than did the equimolar concentration of SO_2." Other animal experiments conducted in 1977 and 1978 by M. O. Amdur demonstrated that short-term exposure to H_2SO_4 at a concentration of 100 micrograms per cubic meter caused increases in airway resistance in guinea pigs.

Recent clinical work with volunteer human subjects, however, has produced more dramatic results. In a series of tests reported in September 1983 in the *American Review of Respiratory Disease*, a group of 17 adult asthmatic patients were exposed by a team headed by Dr. Mark J. Utell to various doses of sulphate aerosols. The patients inhaled measured amounts of sodium bisulphate, ammonium sulphate, ammonium bisulphate and sulphuric acid through their mouths, after which their physical reactions were measured. Each aerosol was inhaled for only 16 minutes, a considerably shorter time than persons exposed to actual air pollution episodes are forced to breathe fouled air.

Despite such brief exposure, "significant responses"—namely, a reduction in the ability of airways to conduct air as well as in the rate of airflow—were observed after exposure to both ammonium bisulphate and sulphuric acid at concentrations of 1,000 micrograms per cubic meter and to sulphuric acid at 450 micrograms per cubic meter. Wrote the report's authors, "We have found that individuals with mild asthma develop transitory airway dysfunction after inhalation of sulphuric acid aerosols. For these asthmatics, there exists a definite dose/response relationship, that is, the higher the exposure level, the greater the airway response." They added: "Sheppard and coworkers (D. Sheppard, 1981) reported that inhalation of 0.5 parts per million of SO_2 during exercise resulted in significant increases in specific airway resistance, whereas exposure at rest had no effect. Perhaps, if our asthmatic subjects were studied at exercise, they might have demonstrated even greater pollutant susceptibility."

Sulphuric acid was found to have pernicious effects in still smaller doses when young people were involved. A University of Washington team headed by Dr. Jane Koenig reported in August 1983 that exposure to sulphuric acid aerosols in concentrations as low as 100 micrograms per cubic meter for only ten minutes after mild exercise produced changes in pulmonary function in ten asthmatic teenagers. The changes included alterations in respiratory resistance, in the volume of air exhaled and in total airflow. According to the researchers, "When exposure to H_2SO_4 was combined with moderate exercise, all the pulmonary functional measurements except functional residual capacity showed significant changes . . . inhalation of 100 micrograms per cubic meter of H_2SO_4 by this group of asthmatic adolescent subjects led to significant changes in pulmonary function. These data may help explain the epidemiologic findings that sulphate air pollution aggravates respiratory disease in asthmatic patients."

Concludes the Congressional Office of Technology Assessment: "Substantial evidence has been gathered indicating injury from some aspect of the sulphate/particulate mix in air pollution. At high exposure levels, sulphur/particulate air pollution can aggravate asthma, chronic bronchitis and heart disease. There is also evidence that sulphur/particulate air pollution causes increased acute respiratory disease in children."

As for nitrogen oxides, the OTA admits that not enough is known "to permit *quantitative* estimation of the health-related damages," but enough studies have been done, including several on human volunteers, to show that the damage is real. Says the OTA:

> Clinical studies of the short-term effects of NO_x on human volunteers have been conducted on asthmatics, patients with bronchitis and healthy subjects. The studies have generally shown that the sensitivity of asthmatics to irritants such as cold air or air pollutants can be heightened by short-term concentrations of NO_2 as low as 0.5 parts per million. . . .
>
> Prolonged exposure to NO_2 has been observed to cause damage to lung tissue in laboratory animals. The principal consequences of such damage appear to be development of emphysema-like conditions and reductions in resistance to respiratory infection. For a fixed dosage, greater concentrations have been shown to cause greater increases in mortality rates for animals exposed to respiratory infection than greater duration of expo-

sure. This suggests that *fluctuating levels of NO₂, such as are found in community air, may prove more toxic than sustained levels of the gas* [author's emphasis].

Epidemiological studies of populations of children exposed to NO_2 concentrations, primarily via indoor air pollution, confirm laboratory findings of reduced resistance to respiratory infection in exposed animals.

Estimating how many people in a given population may be in danger of suffering respiratory damage due to air pollution is far from a simple arithmetic problem, as the American Lung Association admits. Factors such as cigarette smoking, how active people are, age and on-the-job exposure introduce variables that make computations difficult. In its 1983 report on sulphur oxides and public health, however, the association recalled that "while opinions differ on the magnitude of effects, the consensus is that increased air pollution, and in particular increased SO_2 emissions, will be associated with worsened health of the general public."

Some studies have suggested that, under "severe pollution conditions," each increase of 1 microgram per cubic meter of sulphate in the air could cause between 100,000 and 1 million deaths. The various estimates made have for the most part been extrapolated from the number of persons known to suffer from conditions that would make them particularly vulnerable to pollution.

According to the Lung Association, there were more than 16 million reported cases of chronic bronchitis, emphysema and asthma in 1979, any one of which would have been complicated by the effects of oxide pollutants. Approximately 24.6 million people are 65 years of age or older—a stage in life in which lung elasticity is reduced and many people not only have reduced lung capacity but heart problems as well.

Perhaps most sobering is the association's reminder that there are also 46.3 million children under 14 years in the

United States, and that "in very young children the immune system is immature and thus offers incomplete protection from exposure to sulphur oxide gases and particles. In addition, because children spend more time outdoors and are more active than adults, they have greater exposure to ambient air pollutants and, probably, experience greater doses because of higher ventilation rates from heightened activity."

According to reports from West Germany, recent studies indicate a possible link between sulphur pollution and infant crib death. Dr. Wolfgang Baur reported that unexplained crib deaths have been rising in heavily industrialized central Germany, in regions where previous studies have shown correlations between air pollution and greater susceptibility of small children to colds, coughs, hoarseness and intestinal infections.

Baur noted that 80 percent of the analyzed cases of sudden-infant-death syndrome in the area were caused by simple infections of the respiratory system, primarily inflammation of the nose or throat.

In short, the exact number of cases of death or worsened respiratory illness actually caused by sulphur or nitrogen oxides may be unknown, but the potential for trouble is too obvious to be ignored.

An equally great potential for trouble may be lurking in the mechanisms that mobilize toxic metals.

The damage metals can do was first made plain to the general North American public in 1953, when sensational news stories from Japan described the poisoning of the inhabitants of Minamata Bay by methyl mercury, dumped into the water by a local plastics factory. The mercury had been absorbed underwater by various fish and shellfish, which concentrated it in their tissues. When the people of Minamata ate the fish, concentrated doses of the metal averaging between 5 and 20 parts per million entered their bodies.

The results were horrible. At least 44 people died outright and numerous others, their nervous systems ruined by mercury accumulations in their brain cells, were paralyzed for life. Their limbs were contorted like pretzels.

These and other stories, including the revelation in 1970 that high levels of mercury had been detected in fish caught in Lake Saint Clair north of Detroit, sparked the so-called "mercury scare" of the early 1970s. Under heavy public pressure, both governments and industry took steps to eliminate many of the more notorious sources of mercury contamination, such as mercury-based pesticides and the use of mercury compounds in the pulp and paper industry to prevent slime buildup. Permissible dose limits were also set by health authorities, establishing the maximum amount of mercury allowed in human food supplies as 0.5 parts per million.

Whether such dose limits do, in fact, provide an adequate margin of safety for consumers is a question in itself. According to the National Research Council of Canada publication *Effects of Mercury in the Canadian Environment*, a "low level of risk" is considered by some scientists to be one in which "less than five percent of the exposed population" would exhibit symptoms of mercury poisoning. Five percent of the North American population at risk could amount to eleven million people—hardly a "low level."

It is also known that mercury, like many toxins whose effects tend to be cumulative, is eliminated from some body organs more slowly than others. The brain, for example, may retain mercury for much longer periods than the blood or kidneys, and the toxic effects of mercury on brain neurons are irreversible. Thus, even ingested in very small amounts or at irregular intervals, mercury may do great damage over a period of years. As the National Research Council of Canada explains, "The slower mercury elimination rate exhibited by the brain does not allow the mercury concentration in that organ to return to a baseline level. Consequently, successive years of exposure to methyl mercury make it possible to exceed the brain mercury concentration at which nerve cells, especially neurons [essentially nonreplaceable cells] are damaged. Thus, with repeated exposure, the damage may accumulate to a point where sufficient numbers of neurons have been affected to produce clinical manifestations of methyl mercury intoxication.

"An intermittent high level methyl mercury dosage may thus be more injurious than a lower level continuous dosage equivalent on a milligram per kilogram-year basis."

People with already existing nutrition problems, such as Indians in northern Quebec and Ontario whose diets are deficient in thiamine and magnesium, may be more vulnerable than others—vulnerable even to mercury concentrations at or below the presumed safety level of 0.5 parts per million. Unborn children in their mothers' wombs are highly sensitive as well, suffering toxic effects from doses that would be harmless to an adult.

In adults, mercury attacks and destroys neuronal cells in the cerebellum and visual cortex regions of the brain, causing impaired vision, hearing, loss of sensation and eventual coma and death. In the fetus, methyl mercury interferes with the growth of the brain, preventing the migration of developing neuronal cells to their final destination and affecting the brain's structure. The effect can be mild or severe, sometimes resulting in cerebral palsy or microcephaly (shrunken head size).

In the 1970s, of course, once the immediate scare was over it was widely assumed that only a restricted number of people living in areas adjacent to known industrial sources of mercury contamination would ever be likely to be put at risk. To the man in the street, the fate of a small Japanese fishing village or of an Indian tribe living downstream from a pulp mill in some remote Canadian wilderness seemed relatively unimportant. Any haggling over which dose limits would be most likely to protect such people could safely be relegated to the back pages of the newspaper. Acid rain, however, may be introducing a new factor to the risk equation. Scientists have found that acidity, especially the pH of water, has a marked effect on the amount of mercury entering the food chain.

While all forms of mercury are toxic to the human body if they are present in large enough quantity, some forms are more dangerous than others. Methyl mercury is considered one of the most toxic forms, as well as one of the forms most easily taken up by the human body.

Prior to the 1960s, when Swedish investigators proved otherwise, it was believed that insoluble inorganic mercury compounds from industrial sources would simply sink into the mud when discharged in waste water. Swedish researchers found, however, that anaerobic (non-oxygen-using) microorganisms living in lake and river-bottom muds were capable of converting inorganic mercury into organic mono- and dimethyl compounds. The methyl mercury cation CH_3Hg^+ is highly soluble in water, and monomethyls are rapidly absorbed and concentrated by fish and shellfish.

Thus, the presumably inoffensive mercury compounds entering the water from industrial sources as well as mercury deposited with the rain from vapor were in fact being transformed into poison. Rising like a chemical phoenix from the lake bottom, they took on new life, as part of the food chain.

Subsequent investigations have discovered a still more disturbing fact: The so-called "methylation" process is apparently amplified by low water pH. The more acid the lake, the more quickly methyl mercury accumulates in aquatic creatures. Why this happens is still uncertain, but the evidence that it does happen is impressive.

Higher than normal levels of mercury in fish from acidic waters have been measured in Sweden, Norway, Ontario and the Adirondack region of upstate New York. Particularly consistent statistical correlations between mercury levels and pH have been noted in Sweden. In 1980, a Swedish study concluded that extremely few Swedish lakes with pH values below 5.0 contain pike with mercury concentrations of less than one milligram mercury per kilogram of body weight. The normal level for pike at pH 6 was set at approximately 0.6 milligrams per kilo of body weight. In 1981 another Swedish group reviewed the statistics for 152 lakes over a ten-year period and found that mercury level in pike muscle was inversely correlated with water pH. The analysis was complete enough to allow researchers to conclude that a one-unit decrease in water pH would raise the amount of mercury in the muscle tissue of pike by 0.14 parts per million. Additionally, the authors of the U.S. Environmental Protection Agency's report on acid deposition call attention to the fact that "studies in Canada have also found a statistically significant inverse correlation between water acidity and mercury levels in fish," while investigators in the United States were able to establish "a graph of mercury levels in brook trout muscle as a function of fish length for Adirondack lakes [which showed that] fish from acid drainage lakes in general had higher mercury levels."

When excess mercury levels were discovered in fish caught in the English/Wabigoon River system in northern Ontario, local Indian groups were warned not to eat fish. When high mercury levels were found in other Ontario lakes and rivers, the provincial government responded by publishing its *Guide to Eating Ontario Sport Fish*, described in Chapter Two, which warned anglers throughout the province not to eat fish caught in certain heavily contaminated waters.

As the environment continues to acidify, and the mercury levels in fish all over eastern North America rise steadily, it seems a natural question to ask whether, sometime in the next few years, the governments of the United States and Canada will be warning their citizens not to eat fish caught anywhere east of the Mississippi.

Scientists studying the health effects of metals in recent years have also linked serious—sometimes fatal—disorders to the presence of aluminum in the environment. Aluminum toxicity is suspected of being the cause of "dialysis dementia," a disease that has killed several kidney dialysis patients, as well as of being an aggravating factor in cases of "senile dementia," better known as Alzheimer's disease.

An editorial in the 6 October 1978 issue of the *Journal of the American Medical Association* summed up the facts on dialysis dementia in what were, for the normally staid AMA, surprisingly frank and emotional terms. It was obvious from the tone of the article, written by Dr. Samuel Vaisrub, that the association was in deadly earnest: "No less perilous than stormy seas are the waters that reach our 'sea within' by the oral or parenteral route. Some hazards, such as contamination by bacteria, are well known and are often guarded against. Others, such as excess or deficiency of some solute, are still in the realm of investigation. Still others are in gray zones of suspicion and conjecture.

"Emerging from the area of conjecture into that of investigation and near-certainty is a relatively recent danger that lurks in the water of dialysis. Impressive evidence has accumulated to incriminate aluminum in the causation of dialysis encephalopathy with dementia (dialysis dementia, dementia dialytica) as the striking manifestation."

Symptoms of the disease, described by clinical observers, include various brain abnormalities, speech disorders, epilepsy-like seizures and, finally, death.

Vaisrub pointed out to his doctor-readers that for years there had been reports of kidney patients dying from this syndrome, but that "none provided a clue to the mechanism of this com-

plication until Alfrey et al. demonstrated in 1976 a higher content of aluminum in the brain grey matter of 12 patients with
encephalopathy." The findings of other researchers, who also
found elevated levels of aluminum in the brains of stricken patients, corroborated Alfrey's work. Epidemiologists began putting together a statistical case implicating aluminum as well. In
Scotland, for example, it was found that the dialysis dementia
syndrome was "confined to three geographic areas with greatly
increased concentration of aluminum in the water supply," and
that the aluminum in the water "correlated well with the aluminum concentration in the serum of the affected persons."

Report followed report, several of them coming from the
United States. As Vaisrub noted: "Dunea et al. report from
Chicago an outbreak of dialysis dementia affecting 20 persons
between 1972 and 1976. This period also coincided with a
change in the method of water purification that resulted in
higher aluminum levels in city water. Rozas et al. report from
Alma, Michigan, an outbreak of encephalopathy that affected
eight of 34 patients in a small dialysis unit. No further cases of
encephalopathy were noted among 29 patients after the subsequent reduction of aluminum content of the dialysis water
with the use of a deionizer.

"With the bulk of evidence incriminating aluminum, the
door is left open to effective prevention of the dreaded dementia dialytica."

The AMA's message could not have been plainer. It was a
clear vindication of the stand taken six years previously by a
group of Israeli physicians who had studied the syndrome in
rats and warned that aluminum salts, which were prescribed
as part of the treatment of some patients with kidney failure,
should *not* be administered. Far from improving the patients'
conditions, the Israelis said, aluminum salts might be toxic.
The Israelis based their recommendation on a series of experiments with rats that had exhibited "bleeding, lethargy, an-

orexia and death" after drinking aluminum chloride and aluminum hydroxide.

The Israelis' warnings, however, were largely ignored, prompting them, when Alfrey's work with human subjects was published in 1976, to send a somewhat bitter letter to the editor of the British medical journal *The Lancet*. Wrote Israel's Dr. G. M. Berlyne: "Had our advice been taken some years ago, some patients might not have developed dialysis dementia." He did not need to add that several lives might have been saved.

Researchers reporting evidence of the effects of acid deposition today are often confronted with a similar inertia.

Unlike dialysis dementia, which only affects kidney patients, Alzheimer's disease is found throughout the general population. Popularly referred to as "premature senility," it is specifically a disorder of the nervous system, attacking the brain. Its effects have been described as "exquisite emotional torture" for its victims and their families.

When it struck Detroit's Primo Nini 14 years ago, the symptoms were deceptively mild: minor lapses of memory, temporary confusion over the smaller details of everyday life. He had trouble, for example, handling money, leaving his change on the counter at the grocery and forgetting where a $10 bill had gone. Employed as a tool inspector, he managed to keep his job for four years after the onset of the disease. But eventually his failing memory became too big a handicap. When his plant shifted to metric measure, he was unable to master the new system.

One day, when he was sent to the shoproom down the hall from his lab with a tool to be remilled, he got lost. He had worked at the plant and travelled the same halls for 41 years. After that incident, he was asked to resign.

At home, his memory began failing even faster. Once when his wife Dorothy called him for dinner he walked into the dining room to his chair but, instead of sitting down, climbed over it and sat facing the wrong way. He had forgotten how to sit. Asked by a doctor examining him whether he had any children, he answered: "No, no kids." In fact, he has four. Attempting to mow the lawn, he pushed the mower through the flower beds. Eventually, says his wife, he became "like a three year old in an adult body."

By the time such people die, they have forgotten literally everything: who they are, how to talk, how to walk, how to use the toilet. And as they decline, they are aware of what is happening. It frightens them and makes their confusion worse. Pleaded Primo to a friend after the incident with the lawn-mower: "I don't know what's happening to me. I can't think anymore."

Inside his brain, the physical manifestations of Primo's disease would by then have been evident. Centered in the neurons of the cerebral cortex, the part of the brain that governs intellectual function, there would have been numerous microscopic clusters of string-like protein filaments, called "neurofibrillary tangles (NFT)." As researchers Daniel Perl and Arnold Brody described such a tangle in *Science* magazine, "The NFT is readily observed with the light microscope after silver impregnation staining and consists of parallel arrays of thickened, coarse, argyrophilic fibers within the neuronal cytoplasm. Studies of tissue obtained at autopsy show a striking correlation between the degree of clinical dementia and the extent of NFT formation."

The sinister tangles multiply, spreading through the cortex area, while the patient worsens. Family members are forced to watch helplessly as a once-independent loved one turns gradually into a virtual zombie.

According to the Alzheimer's Disease and Related Disorders Association, approximately 50 percent of the U.S. nursing home population suffers from this disease. Dr. Dennis Selkoe of the Harvard Medical School has estimated that Alzheimer's kills as many as 100,000 Americans per year.

Exactly why the neurofibrillary tangles develop and what causes the disease is not yet known, but it is strongly suspected that aluminum, specifically aluminum in its ionic form, has an apparent amplifying effect on Alzheimer's symptoms.

"Ionic aluminum, of course, is toxic in itself," says the Canadian Alzheimer's Society's Dr. Robert Hopkins. "It has been fairly recently established that it binds to proteins called histones in the cell nuclei and prevents the genes in the cells from making more protein.

"Normally, the entry of metal ions is regulated by the cell membranes, but in Alzheimer's disease there seems to be a deficiency that way, and the aluminum ions are allowed in. The feeling [among researchers] is not that aluminum is the cause of Alzheimer's disease, but that for some reason Alzheimer's disease causes changes in the cells which allow the toxic aluminum to get in. Once inside, it then kills the cell."

Once the disease and the aluminum ions are present, the process begun may be synergistic, the disease and the toxic metal complementing each other's attacks in a combined assault that is overwhelming to its victim. Numerous examinations of the brain tissues of Alzheimer's victims have shown marked increases in the level of aluminum in such patients' brains, compared to levels in normal populations.

Alzheimer's specialist Dr. D. McLachlan of Toronto General Hospital notes that there are other examples of an apparent link between aluminum and Alzheimer-like diseases, such as the Parkinsonism dementia common among the Chamorro people on the island of Guam.

"These people live on land that is really bauxite ore [the natural source of aluminum]," says McLachlan. "The ones who are susceptible [to the disease] are the ones who drink pond water, which is high in aluminum and low in both silicon and calcium. Aluminum in its ionic forms will bind to many of the same sites as calcium, and the feeling is that the aluminum is being substituted for calcium in these people's bodies."

According to a 1982 report by Perl and Brody, the neurofibrillary tangles of the Guam victims of Parkinsonism dementia contained "prominent accumulations of aluminum." Parkinsonism dementia is also fatal to its victims.

Asked if he would be worried if the amount of aluminum loading in the water supply of North Americans should increase, Dr. McLachlan replied: "I don't think there's any question that if it's aluminum in soluble form, it has a toxic role. If it's in ionic form, then I am concerned. I am quite concerned."

Aluminum is the third most common element in the earth's crust, its volume exceeded only by silicon and oxygen. It has proven to be highly soluble in acidified soils and is present in increasingly high concentrations in waters with low pH. If it can kill kidney patients, speed the degeneration of Alzheimer's sufferers, smother fish and make the roots of trees wither, to wonder whether aluminum is the kind of thing we really want to see concentrated in the water we drink is only prudent.

Of course, mercury and aluminum are not the only metals being mobilized through the agency of acidic deposition. Among others, the ions of cadmium and magnesium are released into the soil solution and, eventually, into bodies of fresh water. In high enough doses, magnesium can cause nausea, malaise, general depression and paralysis of the respiratory, cardiovascular and central nervous systems. According to Luckey, in *Metal Toxicity*, cadmium "is toxic to all tissues. Symptoms of chronic cadmium toxicity include growth retardation, impaired kidney function, poor reproductive capacity, hypertension, tumor formation, hepatic dysfunction, poor lactation and lowered hematocrit levels."

As the Ontario Ministry of the Environment warned residents of the Dorset area recently, acid rain can also affect plumbing, leaching copper from pipes and lead from the solder used to waterproof pipe joints and connections. Dubbed "pipe poisoning" by journalists, this particular mobilization effect has already had far-reaching consequences. It was first noticed in 1979, when New York State Department of Health investigators under the direction of Dr. Wolfgang Fuhs sampled the water from 30 communities in the Adirondack region and found that most of the water sources were abnormally corrosive. Not all were strongly acidic, but nearly all were exceptionally low in buffering capacity. In some residences copper piping was being eroded and copper levels had risen above normal. Lead levels had also risen, in some cases exceeding U.S. health standards.

Fuhs' work prompted Canadian health authorities to investigate conditions in the Muskoka/Haliburton region of Ontario, in 1981. Water drawn through the plumbing systems of cottages was analyzed for cadmium, copper, lead and zinc content. According to the government report that followed, "After a standing time of from two to 12 hours, the first liter of water drawn contained lead and copper at or above the maximum acceptable levels for these elements specified in the 1978 Canadian Drinking Water Guidelines. In one case, after ten days of standing (not an unreasonable period at a vacation cottage) concentrations of 4,560 micrograms per liter of copper, 478 micrograms per liter of lead, 3,610 micrograms per liter of zinc and 1.2 micrograms per liter of cadmium were recorded, these being five times higher than the maximum acceptable levels for copper and ten times higher for lead."

Equally disturbing, and much more definite in their quantification of health and economic costs, were a series of studies between 1980 and 1983 of roof catchment/cistern drinking water systems in western Pennsylvania and Ohio. E. S. Young and W. E. Sharpe of Pennsylvania State University examined systems in 40 homes and found unusual accumulations of both

lead and cadmium in cistern sediments. Their work was reviewed by the Environmental Protection Agency in its report
on acid deposition, which noted that the lead collected in these
cisterns could foul the drinking water of the cistern owners.
"In the systems they studied there were no safeguards to prevent the ingestion of lead contamination," the EPA said.

Young and Sharpe also measured the concentrations of lead
and copper in tapwater that had stood in the cistern users'
plumbing pipes overnight. Observed the EPA review: "In nine
of the 40 systems studied (22 percent) average lead concentrations exceeded drinking water limits (U.S. EPA 1979); copper
exceeded drinking water standards in 11 of the 40 systems. All
of the systems (100 percent) having all copper plumbing
showed an increase in copper concentration in standard
tapwater.

"If the relationship proposed by Young and Sharpe is valid,
increasingly polluted atmospheric deposition would appear to
be responsible for tapwater copper concentrations in excess of
drinking water standards."

Modifications of the systems that would eliminate contamination were estimated by Sharpe to cost a likely $500 to $1,000
per home. The number of Pennsylvania residences needing
such modifications was not stated, but an earlier study in Ohio
had revealed that more than 67,000 homes in that state used
cistern water systems.

The irony of this situation struck the researchers forcibly
when it was realized that the cistern users in several Pennsylvania counties had originally installed their systems to avoid
using local well water, which had been badly contaminated by
acid drainage from area coal mines. Sharpe told journalist Robert Boyle: "Coal mining has polluted the ground and surface
waters so they're unfit to drink, and the people have turned to
the sky as a last resort. It's the coal that's mined in the area and

shipped to power plants that's coming back to kill their last resort."

Copper and particularly lead are both highly toxic to the human body. Copper in sufficient amounts can cause chronic symptoms of fever, vomiting, diarrhea and jaundice. Acute copper toxicity causes hypotension, hemolytic anemia, uremia and cardiovascular collapse.

Lead is one of the most poisonous substances known. As Luckey writes in *Metal Toxicity*, "Lead is a cumulative poison that causes both chronic and acute intoxication. . . . Acute lead toxicity symptoms in man are lassitude, vomiting, loss of appetite, uncoordinated body movements, convulsions, stupor and coma. Chronic lead toxicity symptoms are lassitude and vomiting, but the real danger is subtle and the symptoms take a long time to appear. They are renal [kidney] malfunction, anemia, brain and liver damage, cancer, hyperactivity and general psychologic impairment. Children suffer permanent damage to the central nervous system."

Whether the metals in question arrive as particulates, wafted on currents of air with the smoke from power plants and smelters, or in solution, dissolved from soil compounds by acid groundwater, the result is the same. Because of acid rain, the human body is being forced to support a constantly increasing burden of toxins.

As Luckey points out, the toxins' effects can be subtle. Where the species' breaking point may be located—the point beyond which the slowly accumulating background combination of noxious elements begins to destroy living organs—no one yet knows. But we could find out sooner than anyone expected.

The list of dangers to human health posed by the acidification of the environment is thus a long one, and it is still lengthening. Only recently, researchers at Florida State University and the University of Miami found evidence of a possible link between acidic pollutants and elevated lung cancer rates in certain regions along the coasts of Florida, Georgia and South Carolina.

The constantly high humidity of the air in these semitropical regions, researchers noted, creates an unusual phenomenon that they called "acid air." Pollutants reacting with the water vapor in the air tend to remain ambient for longer periods than they would in a more temperate climate, allowing their chemical products to become highly concentrated. For most people this results in a mild irritation of the respiratory tract, but when other stresses, such as cigarette smoking, are present, the effects are magnified. According to Professor John Winchester of Florida State University, there is a "significant correlation" between acid air and the high local rates of lung cancer.

"People live in that atmosphere. They breathe it, it's normal to them," says the University of Miami's Tim Aldrich. "But in smokers it creates an increased risk."

A Swedish scientist, Professor Torbjorn Westermark, suspects that the tendency of acid deposition to leach metals from soil may include the leaching of radium, and that radium concentrated in aquatic organisms eaten by man could eventually accumulate in human bone marrow, increasing the risk of leukemia.

Investigators in New York suspect that acid deposition may have been partially responsible for outbreaks of infectious gastroenteritis in residents of the Adirondacks. The bacteria that cause the infection are acid resistant, researchers have noted, and their numbers may have risen as less-resistant strains of bacteria died off in acid well water, leaving an environmental vacancy.

Still to be investigated are the possible effects of several pollutants acting in concert, such as ozone and sulphur dioxide, sulphuric acid and hydrocarbons and numerous other combinations. As the National Clean Air Coalition warned in 1983, "When acid rain mixes with other pollutants, the combined effects may be greater than the sum of the effects." The plain fact is that, at this writing, no one really knows what those effects might be. What is known is that they are highly unlikely to be beneficial.

The United Nations World Health Organization, recognizing that good health is a positive state, has defined its opposite—disease—as "the absence of well-being." If such a definition is accepted, then human communities in North America that currently bear the burden of an excessively acid environment already fit the WHO description.

They are diseased, and the prognosis is not good.

Six

No Commercial Use

I t looks and acts like wet cement, gray, viscous and sloppy, oozing over the end of the clattering conveyor belt and falling with a plop, plop onto the hillside below like bucketsful of mud. Only it isn't mud, or wet cement.

It is a mixture of calcium sulphite and calcium sulphate sludge, and in its present form it is about as near to being the world's most useless substance as a soggy gray blob can get.

A large part of Daniel Lambert's day is devoted to producing, handling and storing this material. He thinks about it often, and probably wishes he didn't have to think about it at all. It is a mess. It gives him grief.

Yet he must continue to deal with it, like it or not, day in and day out all year round, for he is operations supervisor of the Conesville, Ohio, electric power plant—the only plant in the American Electric Power Company's seven-state group equipped with a stack gas "scrubber" antipollution system, and what he has left over when this system has finished scrubbing Conesville's stack gases is sludge: streams of sludge, piles of it, acres of it drying and hardening in the sun.

"We produce 3,500 to 4,000 tons of this stuff per day and we haven't found a commercial use for it," says Lambert. "We've given the material to many different people over the years to try to come up with a use other than just fill, and no one has come up with anything that's commercially feasible."

Tall, fair haired and wearing a yellow hardhat, Lambert is standing, as he speaks, on a dusty 20-foot dune of dried sludge, overlooking a wide gray field full of more sludge—60 acres of it, to be precise, stretching away on every side in the bright noonday sun. Not far away, to the left, a brick-red power shovel with a long steel arm is loading scoop after scoop of the gray dust from the hill into the box of a yellow dump truck, to be carted further out into the landfill area and spread more evenly. A bulldozer's rumbling diesel can be heard in the distance.

To the right, a strange, spider-like machine with a single long tube protruding from it like the hour hand of a clock sits in the center of a hole. The circumference of the hole is marked by the ruts from a pair of wheels attached to the bottom of the protruding tube, which allow the tube to move in a circle. The tube is the terminal point of the conveyor belt that transports wet sludge from the plant to the landfill. It has been built to rotate as the belt moves, so that the gray slop it carries can be distributed more widely. All day long the belt clatters forward, bearing its burden of gunk, and all day long the tube turns round and round as the muck falls off the end.

After a few weeks the rotating, spider-like machine has vanished, surrounded by a wall, and the power shovel rolls over on ponderous steel tracks to free it, scooping and dumping.

"In the winter time the sludge freezes on the conveyor," says Lambert. "It layers up until you've got big knots banging into the steel and we have to get what we call a 'hot truck' out here with very hot water to clean off those points. It's gruesome work, because you're spraying water and it's zero outdoors, sometimes below zero. It's rugged, very rugged."

Earlier that morning, Lambert had shown his visitors through the Conesville plant proper, a six-unit, $516-million facility capable of generating 1,884,000 kilowatts of electricity. It is almost as large as the Gavin plant, and like Gavin it burns massive amounts of coal: an average 13,000 tons per day. At 1983 prices of $35 to $38 per ton, the cost of fueling Conesville station is substantial. The cost of keeping it environmentally clean, however, is also high. The lime used in Conesville's scrubbers costs approximately $67 per ton, and for every ten tons of coal burned one ton of lime is used in the scrubbers.

"There they are," Lambert had said, pointing as his visitors stepped with him onto a steel mesh observation platform several stories up in the plant building. Just below were the scrubbers, one each for generating units five and six, and anyone who might have gotten the impression from reading newspaper editorials that scrubbers are relatively minor attachments that can be fitted onto smokestacks like a filter on a cigarette would have been shocked at their size. Supported by a scaffolding of green-painted structural steel several stories tall, they are nearly as large as the generating units whose exhausts they are intended to control. The pair of scrubbers installed at Conesville cost $52 million to build in the early 1970s, and the capital cost for similar units has risen steadily since. Operating costs in 1980 came to more than $17 million.

Basically, a scrubber is a hollow metal cylinder, with one end connected to an outlet where hot gases from the station's burner fires emerge and the other end leading to the smokestack. Sulphur-dioxide-laden gases enter the cylinder at the bottom and rise until, midway along their path, they encounter a thick spray of liquid lime slurry, forced into the cylinder through a line of spray nozzles. The lime and sulphur react chemically to form liquid calcium sulphite ($CaSO_3$), part of which oxidizes to calcium sulphate ($CaSO_4$). The mixture falls back to the funnel-shaped bottom of the scrubber while the purified gases continue on to the stack. The sludge is pumped from the scrubber bottoms to a nearby sludge treatment plant.

At the treatment plant, it is mixed with fly ash and soot (removed from the stack gases at an earlier stage), which thicken it and speed the drying process. It is then fed onto the conveyor belt and hauled to the landfill. In addition to the scrubbers, the pipeline, the treatment plant and landfill, the scrubbing system also includes two large lime storage silos and several holding ponds used in stabilizing the sludge.

Out of a total plant staff of 592 people, 60 are assigned exclusively to scrubber and landfill operation and maintenance. Some of the latter, Lambert noted, have particularly hard jobs. "There are certain nozzles that plug and other parts that will scale as the gases flow through the scrubbers, and you have to clean the scale off," he explained. "We schedule the maintenance at night, when we're off peak load, and shut down one module at a time while the other one keeps running. We have five people who work nothing but solid midnight shifts to do that cleaning. It's very, very rugged because you're going into an environment that's very hot and humid—in the vicinity of 100° F and 90 to 100 percent humidity."

Four nights a week, after midnight when everyone else is home in bed, five people labor inside a hot metal tank, sweat streaming down their faces, so that the air will not be fouled. The nitty-gritty work of pollution abatement is no picnic.

But the most troublesome feature of scrubber technology, aside from its high cost, remains what to do with its by-product, the ubiquitous, ever-increasing sludge.

"If it was pure calcium sulphate, rather than a mixture of 80 percent sulphite and 20 percent sulphate, we could sell it," says Lambert, walking now across the rolling dunes, his boots caked with dust. "Calcium sulphate is nothing more than gypsum. We had a company in the gypsum and plaster business come out and look it over. They came through with a proposal to buy it, but only if we would process it for them into pure sulphate, which we couldn't do at the price they were offering. Natural gypsum can be mined from pure deposits cheaper than we can produce it from the sludge, so the plan isn't economically feasible."

The sludge coming from the scrubbers, he says, is approximately 93 percent liquid. "After it leaves the sludge treatment plant, where additional lime and fly ash are mixed with it, it's 55 to 60 percent solid. It's a very difficult material to handle because it's thixotropic, which means that the more you work it or move it, the less stable it is, and you tend to sink through it like quicksand.

"It looks dry, but if you stamp on it eventually you'll just push your foot right on through because it'll turn to liquid underneath. Until it finally sets and dries, this is the kind of thing you're dealing with. You have to wait for it to set before you can dispose of it."

He pauses, squinting in the sun, like a prospector in the desert who keeps finding sand instead of gold. "It has a neutral pH and is inert. It's not toxic and it's impervious to water," he continues. "It's similar in many of its properties to concrete, but a very low-strength type of concrete. It's not strong enough to be a pavement or to support any stress. It's fireproof and won't break down easily, so it's no good as a fuel.

"It's also a good insulator. We found that out by accident one winter when we had some rain and a hard freeze right after, and some of the ice got buried in the landfill. In July we were building some road through there and we dug up the ice—and it was still ice." He pauses, looking around the field.

"This landfill site will be abandoned in a year. It has about all it can hold. When we started five years ago the site was 30

feet deep and covered 60 acres. We've filled that and we're above
grade now, even though the first couple of years we weren't
going full swing. Every hour we add another 200 tons or so."

The conveyor belt keeps on clattering, the spider machine
keeps on turning and the gray muck keeps on falling with a
steady plop, plop, earning nothing whatever for American
Electric Power but a massive storage problem. It is little wonder that power companies, whose business it is to produce
electricity and make a profit selling it, are not falling all over
themselves in a mad rush to adopt scrubber technology.

Indeed, if the alternatives were not as serious as they are,
few companies would give a scrubber salesman the time of day.

In addition to the physical drawbacks of the scrubbers themselves, both the utility and metal-smelting industries must also
deal with the fact that, thanks to the severe economic depression of the early 1980s, their general financial reserves are low.
Any major spending, including outlays for pollution abatement, may impose a serious burden on firms and regions still
reeling from this latest bust in the recurring capitalist boom
and bust cycle.

In American Electric Power Company's 1982 annual report,
for example, the company's chairman, W. S. White, Jr., told
shareholders:

> The year 1982 was one of our most difficult. Reasonably good
> financial results in the first quarter became progressively worse
> in succeeding quarters as the effects of the national economic
> malaise intensified.
>
> AEP has felt the sting of economic decline to a greater extent
> than most utilities for two fundamental reasons. First, we serve
> one of the most heavily industrialized regions in the nation, and
> major industrial sectors—primary metals and automobiles, as
> well as those industries related to housing construction—have
> been most adversely affected. Second, and at the same time,
> there were significant reductions in our kilowatt hour sales to

neighboring utilities facing similar difficulties in their own service areas. . . .

As a consequence, 1982 operating revenues were below those of the previous year. *It was the first decline in revenues since 1938* [author's emphasis].

Although the economy had begun to show small signs of recovery by mid-1983, AEP and other utilities were likely to be slow rebounding from such hard times.

The metals industries, especially nickel, were in even worse shape, and their long-range prospects seemed downright grim. Inco Limited chairman Charles F. Baird outdid his AEP counterpart in sheer pessimism in his 1982 annual report to shareholders:

> The past year was one of the worst on record for the mining and metals industries. Demand and prices for nonferrous metals, including nickel and copper, declined sharply as the worldwide recession continued unabated.
>
> Nickel demand fell for the third consecutive year, an unprecedented development, to a 1982 level nearly 30 percent below its 1979 peak. Nickel prices were fairly strong through the first few months of 1982, then fell precipitously in the second half of the year. By November the cash nickel price on the London Metal Exchange, a world market indicator, was down to $1.44 per pound, or about the same level as the company's average realized nickel price in 1973. At the same time, unit production costs continued to rise. . . .
>
> Inco incurred a net loss of $204.2 million, or $2.82 per common share. Net sales fell 34 percent to $1.2 billion, reflecting both reduced volume and lower prices. While the company lost $74 million in the first half of 1982, the loss for the second half widened to $130 million as market conditions worsened.
>
> Inco has now incurred losses for six consecutive quarters. As we enter 1983, our markets remain extremely depressed.

The authors of a September 1983 in-depth review of nickel prices and markets in the metals industry publication *CIM Bulletin* had little encouragement for firms like Inco. In "Future of the Nickel Industry in Canada," a three-man expert panel concluded that "for the nickel industry, recovery from the low demand and low price market conditions does not appear probable in the near future."

Noting that the main use for nickel is in stainless steel products, sales of which are a key indicator of economic and industrial health in national and international economies, the authors warned that unless the hoped-for recovery from the worldwide depression is "unexpectedly fast," things were unlikely to improve: "In the longer term, the consensus of opinion among the forecasters is that the annual rate of growth of nickel consumption in the non-communist world will average between two and four percent per year for the next two decades. A return to the six percent annual growth rate [of the 1970s] is considered as improbable."

In short, the industries responsible for the bulk of the SO_2 pollution in the continent's atmosphere are not likely to be receptive these days to calls for increased expenditures of any kind—particularly not for non-revenue-generating projects.

The auto companies, whose vehicles are responsible for most of the nitrogen oxide pollutants entering the skies, are also in poor financial condition. Detroit in the early part of this decade is a virtual disaster area, with record unemployment and bread lines reminiscent of the Dirty Thirties.

In hindsight, it is unfortunate that the industries in question did not take advantage of better times in earlier years to begin abatement programs with funds that were then available. Missed opportunities and a lack of environmental planning seemed the rule at company after company throughout the 1970s. So cavalier were the attitudes of some companies, in fact, that their critics today may be excused a certain skepticism when they hear the cry of financial constraint being raised again. Like the boy who cried wolf, many executives may have trouble convincing people that this time the hungry predator at their door is real. Poor public relations haven't helped matters.

American Electric Power, for example, has repeatedly claimed that the cost of installing pollution abatement equipment on its coal-fired plants would result in unacceptably high costs to its customers in terms of raised utility bills. Rates would have to be raised an average 18.2 percent over five years to comply with one abatement plan, AEP said in a June 1983 report.

Outside analysts contradict such figures, noting that the rate hikes actually required would in some cases be "almost an order of magnitude" less than the AEP claim. But even if AEP's estimate is correct, the company's own advertising claims deflate its hardship argument. In an advertisement in the *Wall Street Journal* of 5 March 1982, AEP boasted that:

> The average residential customer on the American Electric Power System in 1981 used more electricity but paid less for it, per kilowatt hour, than the average consumer over the nation as a whole.
>
> AEP chairman W. S. White Jr. reported that residential customers on the seven-state AEP System paid an average of 4.75¢ per kwh for their electricity in 1981. The average for all customers of all U.S. electric utilities was 5.98¢ per kwh, 25.9 percent higher. . . .
>
> White pointed out that the cost of household electricity today is virtually the same as it was 45 years ago. 'Of course,' White added, 'if one considers the fact that the 1936 dollar was worth much more than the 1981 dollar, today's price is much less than it was four and a half decades ago.

Thus, even if AEP's rates were raised 18.2 percent, they would still be 7.7 percent lower than the national average.

Also insistent in the past that it could not afford pollution abatement was the second-largest electric utility in North America, Ontario Hydro, a Crown corporation owned by the Ontario government, whose sulphur dioxide emissions take second place in Canada only to those of Inco Limited. It is a significant irony that this corporation, which has not installed pollution abatement equipment on any of its coal-fired generating plants, actually pioneered in the development of scrubber design.

As author Lawrence Solomon recounts in *Breaking Up Ontario Hydro's Monopoly*:

> Between 1969 and 1974 a Hydro research team created two small experimental scrubbers to remove sulphur dioxide from the smoke of coal burning plants. To further develop the technology would have required $10 million, more resources than the utility was prepared to pay to develop a product it considered of secondary interest.
>
> The scrubber technology Ontario Hydro developed is now the most popular offered in North America, but it is not sold under Canadian patent. A Hydro engineer took the idea to more receptive markets in the U.S., where they are produced by an American firm. None of Hydro's coal plants have any installed. . . .
>
> According to Douglas Harrison, Hydro's supervising engineer of environmental and inorganic research: "If we had been given encouragement and funds, we probably could have built them in a couple of years. It would have given us a lot of knowledge, whereas now we have to rely on outside sources for a lot of our information. At that time, we were right out there in the forefront of the technology. People were beating a path to our door because we were doing fundamental work that nobody else was doing."
>
> Hydro does not plan to re-enter the field because "it's too late now. The scrubber technology has moved ahead."

The multinational Inco Limited, whose stubborn resistance to pollution control over the past half century has become almost legendary, also passed up a chance in the 1970s to use available funds for SO_2 abatement. At the time, the company was arguing in private meetings with government officials that a reduction in SO_2 emissions from its Sudbury facilities below

3,600 tons per day would cost $300 million, and that it could not afford such an expenditure.

However, as author/lobbyist Michael Perley, an expert on acid rain, points out, the company *was* able to find approximately $270 million in 1975 to invest in the purchase of the E.S.B. Ray-O-Vac battery manufacturing plant in the United States. It also managed to obtain $70 million in Canadian government loans and "commit itself to $1.1 billion in mineral development in Guatemala and Indonesia in the early 1970's."

An action still more coincidental—some critics have said cynical, on Inco's part—was the company's manufacture of metal alloys in its U.S.-based formed metals division. Recalls a former legislative researcher: "I remember in 1979 I was looking through some U.S. Securities and Exchange Commission forms and found some really funny things about Inco. They were reporting that their 'most bullish market' was going to be their formed metals division and I thought, 'I wonder what they make?' They made a thing called Inconel 625, which was an anticorrosion alloy, and guess what they used it for? They sold it to American utilities who had to clean up SO_2 and needed an anticorrosion alloy for [the equipment used in] scrubbing their stacks. So at home [in Sudbury] Inco saved money by not cleaning up and in the States they made a buck off of the guys who had to clean up, by selling them an alloy. I mean, they're a perfect corporate citizen."

Revelation of the alloy sales in the Ontario legislature created a small furor. Said legislator Stuart Smith: "What a company this is! They are prepared to make money on everybody else's cleanups but they are somewhat hesitant to do their own."

It is also sobering, in retrospect, to realize that the money spent on tall smokestacks, which in the final analysis did little more than exacerbate pollution problems, would have bought a respectable amount of scrubber technology if it had been so invested in the 1970s. Inco, for instance, spent three years and $25 million on its Superstack, approximately the same amount that the scrubber on one of AEP's Conesville units cost the latter firm.

Such tales are an excellent illustration of the old saying, if your foresight was as good as your hindsight, you'd be better off by a damn sight. The past, however, is past. What must be done if irreversible environmental damage is to be avoided is not to lament opportunities lost but to find new opportunities. The cost to society of doing nothing is simply too great to be ignored.

University of Wyoming economist Dr. Thomas Crocker attempted to quantify some of those costs, in very rough terms, in a 1980 paper. He produced an estimate of $5 billion as the annual savings that might be realized from controlling acid deposition. He admitted, however, that the variables involved are so numerous that any such estimate was bound to be "no more than an educated guess" and quite possibly a gross underestimate. In fact, he noted, the very idea of an economic estimate could be absurd: "No market exists in which one can purchase insurance on the amenities and life-support services provided by the ecosystems of entire half-continents," he reminded his readers.

The price of pollution control may seem high, but as the Environmental Protection Agency's Douglas Costle testified in 1979, when the U.S. Congress was debating stricter limits on emissions for newly constructed power plants, pollution controls at that time would have increased the electric utilities' annual revenue requirements by only 2 percent—roughly $1.20 per month in terms of the average residential electricity bill.

Prices are different today, of course, but so are some of the alternatives available to industry. In reality, the alternatives have been both economically affordable and numerous all along.

Two alternative abatement methods recognized very early in the acid rain debate were those of coal washing and fuel switching. By itself, each method has serious limitations, but both could be used, along with other options, as partial components in a more general control plan.

Coal washing is already widely practised. Utilities such as American Electric Power Company have actually pioneered in the field, although their initial motives probably had more to do with plant efficiency than with an altruistic desire to reduce pollution. As the author of a recent article in *Coal Courier*, a house organ of AEP's fuel supply division, explained:

> When it became apparent around 1977 that the percentage of time that generating units were available to produce power was declining, the company had to decide whether to add more generating capacity or to buy power from other utilities—both very expensive propositions—or to improve the quality of coal being fed to the generating unit boilers.
>
> At the same time utilities were facing more stringent state and federal restrictions on SO_2 emissions. . . . We decided to improve our coal quality.
>
> When a high ash and sulphur content run-of-mine coal was burned in the plant during 1974–76, unit availability was 60 percent or below. With the burning of a 100 percent washed coal in 1979, availability increased and the units are now available 80 to 90 percent of the time.

As noted in Chapter One, coal washing essentially involves crushing or pulverizing the coal to be burned, passing it through one or more mesh screens and wetting it in order to allow heavy, sulphur-bearing pyrites to settle out from the lighter coal itself. Depending on how thorough the washing and screening operations are, washing can remove between 20 and 40 percent of the sulphuric impurities from some coals. Sulphur that is chemically bonded with the coal, as opposed to physically mixed with it, cannot be removed by this method.

Nevertheless, washing can improve coal quality and help reduce sulphur emissions.

For a system like AEP, which already washes most of its coal, only minor SO_2 reductions can still be achieved by this method. Says AEP secretary Joseph Dowd: "We're already doing fairly extensive coal washing. You can get a ten to 30 percent reduction in SO_2 emissions at some plants and improve the performance of your boilers. But in my view it is only a supplemental abatement strategy."

Other companies, however, could significantly improve their environmental status by making use of the washing option. In 1980, an Environmental Protection Agency expert estimated that only 40 percent of the high-sulphur coal mined in the Eastern part of the United States was washed before burning, and other consultants believed that washing could reduce SO_2 emissions from Eastern sources by as much as two million tons per year.

As Bruce Ackerman and William Hassler note in their book *Clean Coal/Dirty Air*, "The cost of washing high sulphur coal ranges from two to nine cents per pound of SO_2 removed, compared to a cost range of seven to 45 cents per pound for a 90 percent [efficient] scrubbing system."

Fuel switching, the substitution of low-sulphur Western coals for the high-sulphur Eastern varieties burned by most Midwestern utilities, could achieve even greater SO_2 reductions at a fraction of the cost of installing scrubber equipment. The only expense to the buyer would be the slightly higher cost of shipping the coal east from Western mine sites.

Unfortunately, the high environmental potential of fuel switching is sharply limited by a number of political and social realities. The first and most obvious of these is that any sudden, wholesale change to Western coal would throw thousands of Eastern miners out of work and wreak economic and social disaster on communities throughout such high-sulphur-coal-producing regions as western Kentucky, Illinois and Indiana.

From the utilities' point of view, fuel switching is a more cost-effective option than installing scrubbers, capable of yielding significant pollution reductions at little cost. But they have nevertheless ruled it out as a general solution. As AEP's Dowd says: "We just don't think, as a practical political matter, we would ever be permitted to switch away en masse from our historic fuel supply to western coal. There are communities in Ohio, West Virginia and Pennsylvania that are totally dependent on high sulphur coal. The amount of human suffering and economic dislocation that would be created [by switching supplies] would be absolutely devastating."

In addition to this social constraint, there is also the fact that sections of the U.S. Clean Air Act require newly constructed power plants to meet federal air standards with the "best system of emission reduction" available. In practice this has been narrowly interpreted to mean the most technologically advanced system, which at this point means scrubbers. The political battle sparked by this requirement is still raging and has provoked a deep rift in the U.S. coal mining industry. As Ackerman and Hassler explain, "Once the eastern utilities are forced to install scrubbers, it would be possible for them to meet the [standards] while continuing to use cheap high-sulphur coal. Only if utilities were allowed to substitute low-sulphur coal for scrubbers would a shift away from high-sulphur products be conceivable. Thus it made sense for dirty coal producers to abandon their campaign to weaken pollution standards and take up the cudgels for the costliest possible clean air solution—universal scrubbing." More factors come into play, however, the authors point out: "From the point of view of the United Mine Workers Union, the issue was particularly straightforward. Because its membership is concentrated in the east, it had no difficulty coming out publicly for universal scrubbing. . . .

"Since western [mine] owners were naturally interested in maximizing sales of low-sulphur coal in the east, they would not take kindly to the national lobby endorsing a requirement that would freeze them out of a potentially rich market."

Fuel switching, then, is unlikely to be adopted on a widespread basis. But on a limited basis, during periods of high electrical demand, called "peak load," for example, it can still be a choice for some areas.

Scrubber technology, coal washing and fuel switching do not exhaust the abatement possibilities available for consideration. Other possible methods of emission reduction that might be economically feasible now or in the future include the use of still newer technologies, such as fluidized-bed combustion, ocean thermal-energy conversion, chemical coal cleaning, coal liquefaction and gasification, a change in the scheduling of electrical load transmissions from the so-called "economical dispatch" basis to some combined version of economical and "least emissions dispatch" plans, the use of such nonpolluting electricity sources as "micro-hydro" dams and, last but far from least, a more concerted effort at energy conservation.

The basic engineering principles of fluidized-bed combustion have been demonstrated since 1921. Essentially, the process involves burning coal on a floating bed of limestone and capturing the energy in the resulting steam and exhaust gases. As the coal burns it reacts with the limestone to form gypsum, which can be removed and sold. The process is more energy efficient than conventional coal burning and also tends to minimize production of nitrogen oxides, because it is conducted at relatively lower temperatures. Several fluidized-bed plants have already been constructed in Europe, and a pilot plant is operating in West Virginia.

Ocean thermal-energy conversion (so-called because early prototype versions utilized seawater) is a much newer and less-tested process. It involves the cycling of a substance such as ammonia through heat exchangers whose temperatures are regulated by passing water or other substances through them. If the temperatures at opposite ends of the cycle differ by 25° F or more, the ammonia can be vaporized at one end and used to drive a turbine, then condensed in the cooler end and re-cycled. Employed using the gases in smokestacks, where temperature differentials may be as high as 220° F, the process could be used to simultaneously convert normally wasted heat energy to electric power and cool the stack gases enough to produce saleable sulphuric acid as a by-product. Plans to develop such a system for U.S. utilities were rejected recently by the Edison Electric Institute but could still be revived.

Chemical coal cleaning is a more sophisticated method of coal washing by chemical means that can employ electron beaming, microwaves or hydrothermal reactions. All three means are capable of removing not only pyritic sulphur but chemically bonded organic sulphur as well. Of the three, only the microwave method is expected to be commercially available in this decade.

Coal liquefaction and gasification, which involve conversion of solid coal to either a liquid or gaseous state before combustion, have both been extensively investigated by major energy companies and found practical in various applications. Both result in greatly reduced sulphur emissions when their products are burned. Gasification was used extensively by Germany during World War II, to help offset wartime oil shortages.

"The making of coal synthetics requires the capture of almost all pollutants; otherwise they 'poison' the catalysts," says National Coal Association spokesman Dr. Joseph Yancik. "To the extent that the nation's coal burning facilities switch to synfuels [such as liquid coal or gasified coal], air pollution will be reduced." The chief drawback to the latter options appears to be the relatively high cost of both manufacturing the fuels and conversion to burn them in power applications.

Reorganizing the dispatch systems used by utilities to allocate electricity could also help reduce pollution. Currently, many firms use the economical dispatch system, in which electricity produced in those plants in the grid that are cheapest to operate is sold first. Only when demand outstrips these plants' output are more expensive plants put "on-line" to take up the slack. In practice, however, this system frequently means using older, dirtier plants as the first line of production and newer, perhaps scrubber equipped, plants only as backup. Because the dirtier plants are cheaper to operate, they are used more often and thus pollution is increased.

A least-emissions dispatch plan, as its name implies, would turn the process around, requiring a system to use those plants first that produce the least pollution, while reserving the older, dirtier plants only for backup at times of peak load. Obviously, to move to such a plan permanently would place a utility in the position of being deliberately inefficient. As AEP's Dowd says: "That would be turning the system on its head, economically." The lack of efficiency, however, would last only as long as the older plants were still in service, or until they had been retrofitted with antipollution equipment. When the overall economic costs to society are weighed in the balance, it may be preferable to allow a temporary inefficiency in the grid, rather than an environmental disaster outside it.

As for nonpolluting energy sources, such as small and microhydro dams, their incorporation into power grids could do much to lessen the need for new coal burning plants, as well as the amount such plants must burn during periods of peak load. The technology of water power is well known; it is as old, in fact, as the utility industries themselves. Additionally, the potential sites for smaller dams are encouragingly numerous, and the law, at least in the United States, now provides a framework for action. By its very nature, small hydro is also among the lowest-cost options available—an advantage a utility industry reeling from the astronomical construction cost overruns and massive accident clean-up expenses of its nuclear power projects would do well to notice.

"Small" and "micro-hydro" refer to small-sized hydroelectric dam sites, ranging from 100-megawatt municipal dams down to 2-megawatt or less micro-hydro generators on rural sites. There are literally hundreds of such sites in nearly every state and Canadian province. A recent survey in Ontario, for example, found that 571 locally operated small-scale dams had been abandoned or decommissioned as Ontario Hydro's grid expanded. In addition, the survey found, another 500 sites without existing dams had high potential for development.

The picture is similar throughout the United States. As Paul McKay writes in *Electric Empire*:

> In one case a crafty old Yankee entrepreneur bought a decommissioned 600 kilowatt station at an auction in New Hampshire for $52,000 and six months later was selling his electricity back to the very utility which had abandoned the site in 1975. In Lawrence, Massachusetts a 131 year old flood control dam was converted into a hydroelectric power unit that can provide enough electricity to serve a city of 12,000 and displace several million gallons of oil annually. In New York state the Energy Research and Development Authority identified 1,600 micro-hydro sites that could provide over 3,000 megawatts of electric power. More than one third of these potential sites still had existing dams and headponds.
>
> This is only a fraction of the U.S. total. In fact, a 1977 study prepared by the U.S. Army Corps of Engineers concluded that the United States could double its present hydroelectric output with a program of retrofitting and redeveloping existing small-scale dams, representing an energy output equivalent to 100 nuclear reactors.

Under the Carter administration, legislation was passed requiring American utilities to accept small hydro projects into regional grids and pay their owners for the power they produce.

Water power, of course, creates no sulphur dioxide gas, and every megawatt so produced reduces the amount of power that must be generated by coal-burning plants.

Still more likely to reduce power needs is a realistic commitment to energy efficiency—a concept given considerable lip service since the OPEC oil embargo of the 1970s but accorded nowhere near the practical application its potential deserves.

One concept that has already demonstrated enormous potential, and which could produce enormous real savings if encouraged by a government truly committed to energy efficiency, is industrial "co-generation." Co-generation refers to any industrial system that produces both heat energy, normally in the form of steam, and electricity from the same fuel source, thus doubling the usefulness of the fuel.

An example of how the process works can be seen at the Dow Chemical Company petrochemical refining complex near Sarnia, Ontario, where large quantities of steam are used to refine chemicals. Because the steam produced was actually hotter than needed for the refining process, a considerable amount of waste heat was generated. As Paul McKay describes it: "Dow took ingenious advantage of this inefficiency by installing a high pressure steam/electric turbine halfway between the boiler and the industrial drive. This allowed normally wasted energy to be converted into electricity."

A simple, logical step, the installation of the turbine paid dividends on a scale no one had expected. "Where Dow had once drawn immense amounts of electricity from the Hydro grid, the co-generation system now provides not only all the electricity for the huge complex itself, but has also created a base-load surplus to sell to Ontario Hydro. Unfortunately, Hydro refused to purchase the electricity from Dow."

The widespread adoption of co-generation schemes by companies in the refining, metal smelting and pulp and paper industries, all of which employ large volumes of industrial heat, could produce thousands of megawatts of clean power.

Consumption of power by residential users could also be made much more efficient, reducing the amount of power used without reducing anyone's living standards. Aside from the widely advertised savings to be gained from home insulation, passive solar hot-water heating and other popular options, millions of additional watts could be saved by the simple means of making residential appliances more efficient. The addition of insulation to kitchen ranges and refrigerators is only one of many steps that could be taken to improve performance.

According to a 1976 study that compared appliance efficiencies over the years, kitchen ranges, refrigerators and television sets deteriorated in efficiency between 1950 and 1980. Notes McKay: "The average refrigerator used 345 kilowatt hours per year in 1950, while a frost-free refrigerator built in 1969 used 1,761 kilowatt hours per year. The older refrigerator is insulated and requires manual defrosting once a month, while the newer one has no insulation, requires no defrosting and manufactures perfect ice cubes. Yet the difference in operating costs over 20 years would be $900 more for the modern unit at 1982 electricity prices."

The Harvard University Business School, in a 1979 report on energy, *Energy Future: Report of the Energy Project* summed up the potential of conservation in strong terms: "The United States might use 30 to 40 percent less energy than it does with virtually no penalty for the way Americans live— save that billions of dollars will be spared, save that the environment will be less strained, the air less polluted, the dollar under less pressure, save that the growing and alarming dependence on OPEC oil will be reduced, and western society will be less likely to suffer internal and international tension." It goes without saying that there would also be a lot less acid rain.

There are still other options to examine. For example, despite such graphic demonstrations as that at Three Mile Island, there are diehards in both government and industry who regard nuclear electricity as a still-viable energy strategy. Some nuclear proponents even try to portray nuclear energy as the only alternative to acid rain. Ontario premier William Davis, for example, once told a reporter: "Fine, disagree with nuclear power, but don't come complaining to me about acid rain."

The premier, whose personal friends and Conservative Party contributors include the chairman of the heavily nuclear Ontario Hydro corporation and the major shareholder in the uranium-producing Denison Mines, was voicing an argument that is attractive chiefly to utilities that have already sunk so many billions into nuclear plant construction that they find themselves financially unable to backtrack. Like a gambler who has lost everything he owns, yet despairingly tries for one more roll because he knows he can't cover his debts, they are locked in.

Both the economics of the marketplace and the mounting evidence of the adverse health effects of even low-level radiation, however, are making it increasingly difficult to defend the premier's position. Tales of nuclear disaster, financial and otherwise, have followed one upon the other, from Washington to Pennsylvania, for more than a decade. A typical story is that of Michigan's Consumers Power Company, reported last year in the Detroit papers. The utility has been pushed to the edge of destruction by the burden of a nuclear power plant under construction at Midland, Michigan.

Wrote *Detroit News* reporter Michael Robinson:

> The Midland nuclear power plant is such a severe financial
> burden to Consumers Power Co. that Wall Street analysts and
> energy specialists now question whether the entire project will
> be completed.
>
> They suggest that Consumers, Michigan's largest public util-
> ity, will not have the financial means to finish both the nuclear
> reactors under construction. . . .
>
> The potential impact on the company is damaging its stand-
> ing on Wall Street. A major brokerage is telling its clients to sell
> or avoid Consumers stock. Bonding companies now rate Con-
> sumers among the lowest of the nation's public utilities, making
> it difficult and expensive for the company to raise cash.
>
> The Jackson-based utility's common stock and more than a
> dozen of its preferred stock issues dipped to 12-month lows last
> week. In addition, underwriters last week postponed a plan to
> raise fresh capital by selling two million shares of preferred
> stock.
>
> There are other troubles, ranging from investor lawsuits to
> construction delays and the pullout of a major Consumers in-
> dustrial client. The company is coping by laying off employees
> and cutting its budget and by submitting a $776.6 million rate
> hike request to the Public Service Commission.
>
> "Those guys are in very, very serious trouble," observes Irvin
> C. Bupp, a specialist in utility financing at the Harvard Busi-
> ness School.

Noting that Consumers' problems were typical of other utilities caught in the nuclear trap, Robinson explained:

> The Midland plant was conceived 14 years ago to provide
> low-cost electricity by 1975 for many of Consumers' 1.3 million
> electric customers. The projected price tag: $339 million.
>
> But the plant has suffered cost overruns, escalating construc-
> tion costs and a serious engineering problem caused by soil
> shifting under buildings at the site. The company now hopes to
> complete one nuclear unit at the Midland complex—still just
> 83 percent complete—by mid-1986 at a cost of $4.43 billion.

At that rate, Midland will account for half of Consumers' plant asset base. The company already has an estimated $3.21 billion tied up in the project.

Adding a final touch of irony to the picture, Consumers executive vice-president Walter R. Boris actually used the gambling analogy to explain the situation. "We are now betting the company on this project," he said.

Stories like this bear out the contention of industry critics that nuclear electricity, if used as the alternative to coal, would amount to "the most expensive pollution abatement method of all time." The expense would not be limited to dollars and cents, either, but would include a potentially massive environmental and human health cost.

Numerous radiation scientists such as Dr. Ernest Sternglass, in *Secret Fallout*, epidemiologists such as Dr. Rosalie Bertell and Dr. Thomas Mancuso, and physicians such as Dr. Irwin Bross and Dr. George Wald have revealed the health hazards of radiation. Their work is still controversial, but even a mere possibility that an accident such as Three Mile Island may have been responsible for the deaths of hundreds of children, as Sternglass charged in his 1981 exposé, should prompt society to "err on the side of caution" where nuclear power is concerned.

As Paul McKay writes, a massive switch from coal to nuclear power "would involve little more than exchanging one kind of pollution for another."

Perhaps the best attitude for a company to take when faced with the choices posed by the acid rain phenomenon is that exemplified by Toronto-based Kidd Creek Mines Limited, a mining and smelting firm whose problems are, in many ways, similar to Inco's, but whose management philosophy is light years removed from that of its competitors. The Kidd Creek philosophy, which governs every aspect of company activity, has proven not only socially enlightened but profitably efficient as well.

Where Inco has one of the worst industrial safety records on the continent—71 workers were killed between 1960 and 1974 at the company's Sudbury operations—Kidd Creek has one of the best. There has never been a fatality in a Kidd Creek mine, and its nonfatal injury record is approximately ten times better than the average for Ontario metal mines. Inco has been plagued by lost production due to high absenteeism and long, bitter strikes, some lasting eight or nine months. Kidd Creek's absenteeism rate has averaged between 3 and 4.5 percent, one of the lowest in the industry. Not only has the company never had a strike, it doesn't even have a union. A high-profile employee relations program that gives workers a share in both plant decision making and company profits has kept morale so consistently good that the staff has not felt any need to organize.

The positive approach shown in Kidd Creek's dealings with employees is carried through in its environmental and energy-use planning, as well. In contrast to Inco, the continent's single worst source of SO_2 pollution, Kidd Creek's operations are between 98.3 and 99.6 percent efficient in recapturing SO_2 emissions, which the company processes into saleable industrial-grade sulphuric acid. Using a sophisticated combination of co-generation schemes similar to Dow Chemical's Sarnia plan, it has also come close to energy self-sufficiency in many of its operations, drastically cutting its overhead costs.

Kidd Creek chairman P. Ray Clarke explained the rationale behind his company's way of doing business at a 1982 seminar at Queen's University in Kingston, Ontario, titled "Acid Rain Controls and the Economics of the Canadian Nonferrous Mineral Industry." His audience was made up largely of businessmen and engineers, and his terms of reference were adapted to his listeners. He spoke in a language practical people could understand.

"Believe me, we at Kidd Creek Mines examined this question [of acid rain], we took a hard-headed view," Clarke said. "We also had a rational sense of stewardship toward the present and future community because we are family people, each with several hostages to the future in the form of children and grandchildren. We want them to have a liveable world. Within that framework of management attitudes, we did some comparison shopping a few years ago, aided by a group of experts. . . . We went shopping for the best way to convert a great deal of copper concentrates over many years into marketable metals. The goal was to guarantee that Kidd Creek ore could get to market readily and reliably at the most reasonable cost.

"We decided the *most efficient thing to do* was to spend $300 million on an environmentally clean, truly new plant near our mine [author's emphasis]."

Part of the efficiency, he continued, would accrue from avoiding the future costs of a belated compliance with environmental regulations, and part would stem from internal conservation of the company's own energy resources.

He asked his listeners to ponder: "According to a House of Commons subcommittee, cutting the emissions of one source of sulphur dioxide by half would, by one estimate, reduce health costs by $500 million a year. Then you think about how desperately the treasurer of Ontario, the Minister of Health and the federal government are wrestling with the cost of health and how it will be met. . . .

"Emission control is a relatively low cost insurance premium. Being well ahead of the regulators will, I suggest, become recognized as the only prudent place to be."

Noting that the firm's acid-manufacturing plant, sited near

its copper smelter, cost approximately $14.5 million to build, he then worked out the economics of its operations in detail: "Operating costs are reasonably straightforward. A metallurgical sulphuric acid plant uses energy primarily to drive the main blower. That takes 80 percent of the power consumption, which would typically be 100 kilowatt hours per metric ton of acid produced by a double absorption plant. Maintenance costs amount to between five and six percent of the installed capital cost. For our copper smelter acid plant, that would be equal to approximately $3 for a metric ton of acid. Operating labor and supplies would require another $2 a ton. If electrical cost is assumed to be 30 mills per kilowatt hour, all these outlays come to about $8 to produce a metric ton of 100 percent basis acid. That estimate assumes full use of the plant. If acid sells for, say, $10 a metric ton, clearly the product pays for the operating but leaves little cash flow to contribute to capital or profit. Our copper smelter acid plant capital cost of $14.5 million plus $3.2 million capitalized interest, over 20 years, would amount to $4/ MT of 100 percent acid. So the losses are marginal."

Assuming that pollution controls become mandatory, the fact that compliance with them could be had at only "marginal" cost is a positive factor in itself. But Clark then proceeded to demonstrate how the overall system was actually saving money for Kidd Creek: "Let me review some of the advantages we have found. Of course, some of these might be available in the old polluting-type smelter, but let us assume that we are in the 1980s and you would not be allowed to build such a plant.

"Sulphide concentrates are fuel. Since we will burn about 500,000 tons of concentrates per year, we have theoretically the energy equivalent of 370,000 barrels of oil. A large percentage of the heat from the roasters and furnace is available as high-pressure steam, which is a source of power. We use this in steam turbines to drive pumps, fans, etcetera. The process itself requires heat, and therefore low-pressure steam is used in heat exchangers. Most of the remaining heat is used for space heating. We use hot water from copper furnace cooling to raise the temperature of the concentrator flotation circuits to 80° F. This improves recoveries, particularly in winter, increasing operating income by $2 million per year. With an integrated operation such as ours, savings of $1 to $2 million per year can be made by smoothing out electricity demand peaks between the various plants by the controlled use of firm and interruptible power."

There are, he continued, other advantages as well. "The use of interplant products is also cost-saving. High zinc and lead flue dust from the copper smelter is treated and metal values recovered in the zinc plant; copper cake from the zinc plant is treated with the copper recovered in the copper smelter, and so on.

"One of the major reagents in the concentrator is copper sulphate to activate sphalerite in the flotation process. It was once purchased, but we now make it from a copper precipitate produced in the zinc purification stage and our own sulphuric acid. This gives us a substantial saving in concentrator operating costs of about $1 million per year."

Operation costs, too, are affected. "The use of slag from the new copper smelter for backfill underground will reduce mine operating costs. In finely ground form it can be used to replace a small portion of the purchased Portland cement. In its own granulated form it will replace some sand which presently has to be quarried. The value of this is $1 million per year."

Finally, "A quite significant economic advantage is also found in reduced organizational requirements. To expand existing services both human and physical, such as maintenance, engineering, administration, electrical, water supply, natural gas, effluent and solids disposal from a fixed base is much less costly than having each production unit at a separate location. These advantages are difficult to evaluate precisely, but should amount to many millions of dollars per year."

The plant, in short, is a masterpiece of integrated, whole-systems planning in which each component interlocks with its counterparts to form a vital circle. It is much like the natural ecosystem, which it does not harm.

Kidd Creek, of course, is not the only smelter company that could recover marketable sulphuric acid from its emissions, nor is acid the only end product that could be obtained. As Ross Howard and Michael Perley recount in *Acid Rain*, Inco could also produce sulphuric acid, and in the past it has done so. Until the 1970s, when a constriction in markets for sulphuric acid prompted the company to cease making it, Inco was selling as much as 1,400 tons of H_2SO_4 per day to the chemical company CIL Limited.

The nickel company was reluctant to resume acid production when a government study team suggested it in 1975, although a possible key to making production more consistently profitable had been found in Cargill Township, a wilderness area near Kapuskasing, Ontario. According to federal and provincial government reports, nearly 62.5 million tons of phosphate rock was located there. Write Howard and Perley: "The phosphate is suitable for making commercial fertilizer by adding one essential ingredient—sulphuric acid. One hundred and five miles south of the untapped Cargill phosphates is an uncontrolled source of immense volumes of sulphuric acid: Inco's Superstack in Sudbury."

Despite government forecasts indicating that the world markets for sulphur and sulphur/phosphate fertilizers were increasing, neither federal ministers nor Inco followed the matter up until 1980. The Cargill deposits were mentioned again then by the federal environment minister as possible elements in a future abatement plan, but no firm dates or commitments were suggested.

According to Howard and Perley, a member of the federal Ministry of Energy, Mines and Resources team that originally helped evaluate the Cargill phosphate potential believed the decision not to move ahead was taken because "Inco sees acid production only as an unprofitable investment, rather than the cost of pollution abatement. It's cheaper for Inco to do nothing."

In 1978, two university business faculty professors, T. F. Cawsey and P. R. Richardson, examined employee relations at Kidd Creek Mining and presented their report at a Queen's University (Kingston, Ontario) seminar on the subject. Although their subject was limited to employee relations, their conclusions had wider significance. Wrote the professors: "The most important factor in the program's success has been the attitude of management and supervision. All other factors can be related to this."

Seven

A Window in Time

In Washington's Congressional pecking order, the Rayburn House Office Building at Independence Avenue and Third Street is Status City. Named in honor of Lyndon Johnson's mentor and idol, former House Speaker Sam Rayburn, the massive, columned structure facing the Capitol houses the offices of the biggest guns in the House of Representatives: the committee and subcommittee chairmen, senior Congressmen with years of experience whose power and influence reach far beyond the confines of the district from which they come.

Two blocks east, at Independence and First Street, is the more modest Cannon Building, facing a Capitol parking lot. It also houses the offices of Congressmen, but not necessarily the famous and powerful. Where the Rayburn Building shelters chiefs, Cannon is occupied by braves, many of them freshmen Congressmen serving their first terms, members of less influential subcommittees or those with low seniority on the most influential committees.

The office of Gerry Sikorski, freshman Democrat from Minnesota's Sixth District, is on the fourth floor of the Cannon Building, but one has the impression that the 35-year-old attorney and former Minnesota state senator is destined eventually for a Rayburn address. He sits as a member on the high-profile Energy and Commerce Committee, a plum assignment for a newcomer, and has established excellent working relations with the chairman of Energy and Commerce's Health Subcommittee, California Democrat Henry Waxman.

Their alliance is natural; Waxman, a strong defender in 1981 and 1982 of the Clean Air Act, helped thwart efforts by Committee chairman John Dingell and the Reagan administration to gut the act and weaken clean air standards. Sikorski, whose home state has a highly progressive record on environmental matters, helped draft Minnesota's pioneering legislation to control that state's acid rain, which was the first such legislation passed by a jurisdiction in the western hemisphere. So strongly identified with the issue is he in Minnesota that the mantle of "Mister Acid Rain" in the House of Representatives fell easily onto his shoulders after the departure from office of former clean air champion and ex-Ralph Nader assistant Toby Moffett of Connecticut.

Together, Sikorski and Waxman have co-authored what may be the only politically realistic plan to control acid rain in the United States, a carefully thought out, balanced bill that could gather the support of all sides in the acid rain debate and, if passed during the "window in time" represented by the current Congress, save not only thousands of lakes but thousands of lives as well. Despite the opposition of the Reagan administration to pollution control, the Waxman/Sikorski Bill, HR-3400, had attracted more than 115 cosponsors by the first week in February 1984, demonstrating unusual popularity among the legislators themselves.

But politics is full of the ironic and the unexpected.

Notwithstanding its support on the House floor, the bill

could fail and the lakes and lives be lost, due in part to the actions of the very environmentalists who first alerted the public to the problem of acid deposition and who want above all else to make the acid rain stop falling.

The paradox is potentially tragic.

"Do you want some pop?" Sikorski asks, holding out a bottle of diet Coke as he sits down on the couch opposite his paper-cluttered desk. He takes a swig from a second Coke bottle in his other hand as his reporter-visitor sets up tape recorder and microphone.

Only moments earlier, a delegation of constituents from Sikorski's home district, apparently union officials, had left, and two more groups of hometown people are waiting just outside his office door to buttonhole their congressman as soon as the reporter leaves. It is nearly one o'clock and Sikorski, in subcommittee hearings all morning, has not yet had time to eat lunch, nor is he likely to eat for several hours.

One of the penalties of elected office is not having a lot of time to breathe, or eat. The pop is a necessary stopgap.

Between swigs, Sikorski tells his tale:

"I spent six years in the Minnesota Senate," he says. "It is a very environmentally conscious state. The environment is not only part of our quality of life but a major part of our economy. We're the Land of Ten Thousand Lakes, tourism is our third-largest industry and produces over 200,000 permanent, full-time jobs. We're talking three-plus billions of dollars annually towards our economy—$600 million this year from sport fishing alone. On opening day in May, one out of every three Minnesotans would be on the lakes, fishing. It's part of our lives.

"When I came here, I wanted to get on Health and Environment because of my interests, and Toby Moffett's files were given to me. Waxman and the others had so many irons in the fire that, when it came to acid rain, they were willing to let me carry the ball."

He pauses, sitting back and gazing reflectively at the ceiling.

"With our bill, we have the best chance at real acid rain control legislation in the Congress. It offers the only meaningful opportunity to control acid rain quickly. It's the first truly national bill on this issue in the history of the Congress, it's meaningful in terms of reduction of sulphur and nitrogen oxides, it safeguards miners' jobs and spreads the financial burden through cost-sharing." He turns, puts down the Coke and looks at his guest:

"But if we don't stir up the pot, we're going to lose it."

The Waxman/Sikorski Bill is, indeed, a balanced effort. It calls for a cut in total annual U.S. emissions of SO_2 and NO_x of 14 million tons—10 million in SO_2 and 4 million in NO_x—a reduction of close to 50 percent.

The reduction would be achieved by requiring the 50 largest pollution emitters burning medium- or high-sulphur coal, most of them in the Midwest, to install stack scrubbers by 1990, thus reducing SO_2 emissions by 7 million tons. In addition, the 48 continental states would be required between them to achieve a 3-million-ton SO_2 reduction from other emission sources using whatever means they choose, from fuel switching and least-emissions dispatch to installing scrubbers.

A tightening of the limits on NO_x emissions for newly constructed power plants, as well as for light- and heavy-duty trucks manufactured after 1986, would bring reductions of 1.5 and 2.5 million tons of NO_x, respectively.

The requirement that the top 50 emitters must employ scrubbers would enable these plants to continue burning eastern high-sulphur coal, thus preserving the jobs of thousands of United Mine Workers. As for the considerable expense to the Midwestern utilities of outfitting their plants with scrubbers, this would be partially offset by spreading it throughout the country via a one-mill-per-kilowatt (one mill equals one tenth of a cent) surcharge on the generation of electricity. This would result in a hike of only an extra 50 cents per month on the average residential utility bill. Utility ratepayers in the heavily industrial states whose plants would be installing the scrubbers—and who have been hardest hit by unemployment in the recent depression—would thus not be forced to bear the full cost of cleaning up.

In short, the bill is a perfect example of "something for everyone" politics, and it is no accident that it is.

"This bill is a product in a sense of the last Congress, where we failed miserably to get acid rain control legislation," explains Waxman aide Jerry Dodson. "We listened to the reasons why and talked to different members to find out what they were willing to do, and then we put something together. That's what this bill is, a result of listening and not talking."

Earlier bills in both the House and Senate had targeted only 31 states for acid rain control and required the states producing the heaviest emissions to bear the greatest share of the clean-up costs. "In the last session people said 'this 31-state approach doesn't make sense, because a power plant in Kansas City, Kansas, can pollute as much as one in Kansas City, Missouri, but one is covered and the other is not.' Louisiana was one of the 31 states and it emits 22,000 tons a year, while Kansas wasn't and it emits 150,000 tons. Explain that to me!" asks Dodson. "The 31-state figure apparently had to do with sulphate levels being higher in those states, but just measuring the sulphate levels in the air doesn't tell you where the sulphates are coming *from.*

"Also, there were no mechanisms in these previous bills for spreading the costs and no mechanisms for protecting jobs. The Midwesterners said 'come on, bring your bill out here and we'll talk about how unfair it is, how our jobs and our economies—100,000 jobs, 200,000 jobs—will be lost.' And that kind of stuff talks on the floor. If you're going to try to beat that back by saying, 'but we need it to protect fish,' you'd better watch out."

The earlier House bill, introduced by Moffett, was essentially similar to the Senate bill introduced by Senator Robert Stafford of Vermont, chairman of the Senate Environment and Public Works Committee. Recalls Dodson: "That kind of bill could have better success in the Senate because the Senate committee at that time had a lot of Westerners and New Englanders, and the bill's impact was on the Midwest. They said, 'let's get together and vote, and the Midwesterners will pay for it.' You could get it through the committee there."

The House committee, however, had several Midwestern members, including the powerful chairman, John Dingell of Michigan. "We were told by the environmental groups that the Stafford Bill was the same one they wanted introduced over here," says Dodson. "That was done by Toby Moffett. And they were saying, the way we'll win is to pass this bill in the Senate and then at conference committee, even though you've lost in the House; we'll agree that the Senate version will be effective.

"Well, we lost miserably in subcommittee and we lost even worse, 25 to 5 in full committee, in the House. The environmental groups didn't care, because they felt they still had their Senate strategy. But the problem was the bill was also going to fail on the floor of the Senate. You can stack a committee, but you've still got to face the floor. And pretty soon they began picking up the indications that they never were going to get that vote off the floor."

The Senate committee may not have had opposing votes, but the Southern and Midwestern members on the floor were no more anxious than their House colleagues to cut their own throats. Dodson continues:

"In this Congress, early in the year, we were told by the environmental groups: 'Introduce the Moffett Bill again and we're going with the same strategy.' We checked with our Senate colleagues to find out whether they had the votes over there for that same bill, and they said no, they didn't."

At that point, as Dodson described, those who wanted the bill began considering it differently. "So we had to strike out in a new direction because we were only going down to defeat again. And how many Congresses do you have to have it rubbed in your nose that you don't have a solution that's going to work?

"Political compromises are the nature of Congress, and anyone who believes that those kinds of agreements aren't made every day up here is dreaming. We can't legislate in a vacuum. Members can't say we're going to get acid rain control and to hell with electric rates and jobs. Those who say you can are not dealing with reality, because there are very powerful members on the other side, opposing it.

"You have Senator Robert Byrd on the Senate side, and it's King Coal in West Virginia. You can't say, 'Bobby, I'm sorry but we're going to flush your economy down the drain because we're going to save some fish in New England.' It's the same in the House. If that's the calculus we're working with, I know where this Congress is going to come down."

Waxman's assessment is virtually identical.

"The Midwestern people aren't going to throw Grandma and Grandpa out on the street with skyrocketing utility rates, or throw their miners and union support to the wind, especially on the heels of a recession which was the worst since the Great Depression, and in which they suffered more than any other region in the country," he says.

The Waxman/Sikorski Bill was accordingly written to take such realities into account, and its success in doing so is measured by the abnormally high number of cosponsors it had attracted by February. It is the kind of compromise bill that could pass on the House floor, and pass by a good margin, with or without White House opposition.

To the chagrin of Sikorski and Dodson, however, citizen and environmental groups objected to the bill and withheld their support. Although it was introduced on 23 June 1983 it did not receive endorsement from any of the major groups until late in October, and even then the endorsement was lukewarm.

The reasons given for this lack of enthusiasm vary, depending on who is asked to explain, but lobbyists for most of the major pressure groups agree at least in part with Sikorski's opinion:

"The environmental groups have held out for a 12 million ton SO_2 reduction, rather than ten million," he says. "They are also somewhat unhappy with the cost-sharing aspects of the bill. Also, I think the President's finesse when he put [William] Ruckleshaus in at the Environmental Protection Agency had an effect. There's a kind of honeymoon period with a new appointee and they may have been looking for an initiative from there. I think he has effectively sidelined the interest groups on acid rain for several months. But he's not going to be able to come up with anything and it looks as though we're back to square one."

The League of Women Voters' Lloyd Leonard insists that the league "didn't oppose" the Waxman/Sikorski Bill, but admits that the bill "does not provide as much sulphur reduction as we would have liked" and because of that "I and various others called up members of Congress and asked them not to cosponsor the bill. With the National Academy of Sciences recommendations it was real clear that we needed more sulphur reductions and that we should go for it, that's all."

The National Audubon Society's Leslie Dach agrees: "We originally didn't feel it was appropriate to encourage cosponsors, since the bill didn't have a satisfactory tonnage goal."

The National Research Council of the National Academy of Sciences had called in 1981 for a minimum reduction of 50 percent "in deposited hydrogen ions" to protect the environment. Although it did not specify at the time how much of a reduction in emissions would be needed to bring about the 50-percent change in deposition, it was widely assumed that a 50-percent emission decrease was required. At the time, the United States was emitting approximately 24 million metric tons of SO_2 yearly, and thus a 12-million-ton decrease was demanded by the pressure groups.

Sikorski himself says he would prefer a 12-million-ton cut in SO_2, but adds: "The Congressional Office of Technology Assessment computer we used shows a very sharp upturn in terms of a graph of costs associated with the last 2 million tons. The average cost-per-ton reduction in the first 10 million tons of SO_2 was around $500 or $600. But to go from 10 to 12 million, those last 2 million tons would average about $2,000 a ton. It's a real jump.

"The Edison Electric Institute [a spokesman for the utilities] has hit the bill as costing not $20 billion, but $200 billion, which of course is exaggerated. But you don't want to give them an issue to pick at. The feeling is that with the $500 or $600 figure you could do a good cost/benefit analysis, whereas you can't if you throw in the last 2 million tons. Our feeling is that [in the end] you could get them in conference committee anyway. So we thought we'd go with something we wouldn't have so much trouble defending."

The strategy, in other words, was to get the bill through the House with a 10-million figure and tack the other 2 million on later, when the weight of the Senate conferees would be behind the move. It made sense to Sikorski but apparently not to the environmental groups, whom he views philosophically.

"They are there to be the pokers and pickers and prodders in the legislative process," he says. "They're there to take the strongest position possible and to make sure the system and the politicians are honest. They don't make you comfortable by taking an absolute position, but they serve a purpose by doing that."

Unfortunately, carried beyond a certain point, absolutism can sometimes become counterproductive. Recalls Sikorski:

"In hindsight, we had everyone running on acid rain back in July and August. We had the National Academy of Sciences' most recent report, the White House Office of Science and Technology report and the media focus, and they [Reagan and the utilities] were on the run." Indeed, the confluence of opinion and public pressure at that point was difficult to resist.

The National Academy's report, *Acid Deposition, Atmospheric Processes in Eastern North America,* had demolished industry claims that there is no connection between individual plant emissions and acid deposition outside a plant's local area. Said the academy: "The [NAS] committee concludes that there is no evidence that the relationship between emissions and deposition in northeastern North America is substantially nonlinear when averaged over a period of a year and over dimensions of the order of a million square kilometers. It is the committee's judgment that if the emissions of sulphur dioxide from all sources in this region were reduced by the same fraction, the result would be a corresponding fractional reduction in deposition."

The White House Office of Science and Technology Policy (OSTP) had been asked to review the current "state of knowledge about acid rain" and to advise the President of their findings. It was assumed by many observers that the nine-member committee appointed for the task in 1982 would come up with findings that reflected the Reagan administration position that not enough is known about acidification to warrant any action. If that was the plan, the scientists failed to cooperate.

The OSTP report surprised everyone, stating that "the phenomena of acid deposition are real and constitute a problem for which solutions should be sought." Worse, the committee directly contradicted previously stated White House positions. Agreeing that scientific understanding of the problem was "incomplete," the committee nevertheless insisted that "Recommendations based upon imperfect data run the risk of being in error; recommendations for inaction pending collection of all of the desirable data entail even greater risk of damage. . . . It is in the nature of the acid deposition problem that actions have to be taken despite incomplete knowledge."

The White House, needless to say, was severely embarrassed, and spokesmen for the Reagan administration took pains to state that the report did not represent an official view. But the damage was done.

"We had major divisions in industry also at that time," says Sikorski. "The public pressure was unbearable and was at the point where a decision should have been made on an issue that's been percolating too long. But it's clear that once again the hard-liners have taken over."

The endorsements of the all-important grassroots pressure groups failed to materialize, and the bill stagnated throughout the summer and part of the fall. Remarked a pessimistic Dodson in October:

"I said three months ago we had a 50–50 chance of getting Clean Air Act amendments in this Congress. Now I don't think the likelihood's there, largely because there's been a failure of the constituent groups to coalesce around HR-3400. As of today, not one group has endorsed the bill. What's happened is that the members are willing to vote and resolve this, but the constituent groups are not.

"The environmentalists want more tonnage, at any cost. The United Mine Workers have locked themselves in the closet. They're hoping a year will pass and no legislation will be enacted. We clearly have the best bill for them, but they won't endorse it. It's the same with the utilities. The chairman of the board of Edison Electric Institute two weeks ago said it's time we stopped letting demonstrators on the streets control our policy! Well, I haven't heard rhetoric like that in 20 years, since I *was* a demonstrator on the streets."

Success had been almost tangible: "We knew the major law firms of these utilities in many cases were recommending they endorse this bill. Then, just as things started to coalesce, the environmental groups, zip, went off in their direction of 12 million tons or bust. Reagan had been under pressure to come up with something [like an administration 'steal their thunder' bill], because things looked like they could move, and then they saw this thing pull all apart and that was it. They saw the splintering and said let's just don't bother."

As Sikorski points out, Congressmen may cosponsor a bill, but if there is no real pressure from constituents in their home districts that sponsorship may melt away, ending as mere lip service to a bill on which no true action will be taken. "Unless there's grassroots support, they'll waffle, waver, wish and wash," he says. "If there aren't the letters or notes or phone calls coming in, they must seriously question if it's an issue. They're going to be hesitant. If I had 100 letters tomorrow in my office on this it would be very impressive. But in this case we're missing those grassroots."

"I feel very strongly about environmental protection," says Dodson. "But I hope I can disagree with my environmental colleagues on this. I think they made a terrible error three months ago by not endorsing this bill and working for it. They could have tried to get additional tonnage down the road, but they're looking for the perfect bill. I think it's very sad because we made a really bona fide effort to get something moving. And you can say it wasn't just the environmental groups, but that's the key."

"If we don't stir up the pot, we're going to lose it for this session of Congress," Sikorski adds. "The closer we come to the presidential election the greater the push will be on candidates, not to resolve the problem, but to use it as an election issue. That's great, to get the issue out there, but I'd prefer to make sure the lakes in northern Minnesota don't get killed in the interim."

"We've had conversations with different presidential candidates' staffs and I can tell you they're not anxious to see this thing resolved either, because they see currency in it," says Dodson. "We have a member from New England who has been running for the last four years on the basis of acid rain control and make the Midwest pay. It's totally unrealistic politically, but why should he give that great issue up in an election year? What's the best thing for him to run against? Some guy from Ohio!"

(Indeed, as subsequent weeks wore on, the Presidential candidates began staking their claims to acid rain as an issue. By January, five Democratic contenders had called for a 50-percent cutback in acid emissions by 1990. On January 9, 1984, in New Hampshire, Democratic front-runner Walter Mondale vowed acid rain control treaties with both Canada and Mexico but warned that the polluters would have to pay. Utilities that burn high-sulphur coal "must not be allowed to pass on their costs to consumers" for cleaning up, he said. Such a position, of course, would never get the vote of an Ohio senator or representative if a future Mondale bill got to the floor of Congress.)

To their credit, by late October 1983 many of the environmental groups began to realize that time was running out if they hoped to get acid rain legislation through the current Congress and that, flawed or not, the Waxman/Sikorski Bill was the most likely vehicle to make the trip through the House of Representatives successfully. An amendment was introduced by Representative Richard Ottinger of New York calling for the addition of 2 million more tons in SO_2 reductions to the languishing HR-3400, and several groups belatedly announced they would endorse the Waxman/Sikorski Bill—still with reservations because the polluters' burden would be shared by the people—as being better than no bill at all. For instance, on 17 October, National Clean Air Coalition chairman Richard Ayres told congressmen: "The National Clean Air Coalition urges you to co-sponsor the Sikorski/Waxman/Gregg Acid Rain Bill, HR-3400. . . . The coalition realizes that HR-3400 is not perfect. But we must begin the move towards implementing an acid rain control program now. Improvements to the bill can be made in coming months."

Such lukewarm support was welcome, but not exactly inspiring. As another Congressional aide put it: "If somebody has been telling you for months that a bill is no good and not to sponsor it, then suddenly reverses course and says, 'hey it's OK after all,' are you going to take them seriously?"

There is, of course, a chance that congressmen will take it seriously, and that the Waxman/Sikorski Bill may yet pass the House in this Congress. If that happens, it must still face a conference committee, in which senators with a much different view of how the law should read will have the opportunity to tear it to pieces. Because the Senate, unlike the House of Representatives, is not elected on a population basis (one representative for roughly every 500,000 voters), but on a basis of equality (two senators per state regardless of population), the power balances there may be radically different.

Says the League of Women Voters' Lloyd Leonard, whose group also changed its mind and decided late in the game to endorse HR-3400: "The Senate won't accept the Waxman/Sikorski Bill. It has been crafted to take care of the people in the House, but in the Senate Wyoming has the same votes as Pennsylvania. The Stafford Bill couldn't pass the House, and the

Waxman Bill can't pass the Senate. If any bill passes the House, the Waxman Bill is going to be it. But I think we're going to have a very interesting time of it after that."

Time, meanwhile, is running out. The presidential election is gearing up, with every indication that acid rain may be turning into a political football. If it is, and the current Congress fails to enact an effective law, a terrible toll may be taken in human lives and environmental damage before a new Congress and a freshly elected president consider the issue again.

If the Waxman/Sikorski Bill or one substantially like it should pass the Congress this session, Jerry Dodson and the congressmen for whom he works won't be the only people celebrating. An immense sigh of relief will also be breathed in Canada—the United States' long-suffering northern neighbor and ally, whose people and economy have served for too many years as an unwilling early warning system, indicating in advance the kind of damage America's pollution will eventually cost its own citizens.

Like a canary in a mine, whose susceptibility to poisonous gas makes it an ideal alarm device for miners, Canada is particularly sensitive to the effects of acid rain. Its geographical location puts it directly in the path of U.S. emissions, and the poor buffering capacity of the granite bedrock of the Canadian Shield renders the eastern half of the country highly vulnerable to damage.

It should be no surprise that when Dr. Harold Harvey and his associates began in 1968 to 1972 to report the impact of decreasing pH on Ontario's lakes, they received more notice than did the Adirondack studies of Cornell's Dr. Carl Schofield in the United States. Heavily dependent on both tourism and the resource industries, the province of Ontario is typical of the nation as a whole. Like Gerry Sikorski's Minnesota, it has a massive stake in tourism, which is the second largest industry in the province. Annual revenues from tourism average $5 billion, and more than 470,000 Ontario jobs are directly related to it. The Muskoka/Haliburton area alone reaps $200 million yearly from cottagers, while sport fishermen added more than $450 million to the provincial income in 1975. Tourism is nearly as important to Quebec and the Maritime Provinces, as well.

As for forestry, Canada is the world's leader in the production of newsprint and second in output of paper pulp. One out of every ten Canadian jobs is directly or indirectly connected to the harvest and sale of trees, which in 1978 accounted for $18.5 billion in shipped goods and $9 billion in value added to goods by processing. The net contribution of forestry to Canada's balance of payments in that year was $10.6 billion.

Canada is likely to feel even more threatened by any danger to its agriculture, which is sharply confined not only by the shorter northern growing season but by the limited amount of available farmland. Ninety-five percent of Canada's land mass is either not tillable at all or subject to such severe soil and weather restrictions as to rule out growing most major crops.

The tiny percentage of Class I and II farmland, the kind of soil best suited to agriculture, is concentrated along the U.S./Canada border in the wheat-growing Prairie Provinces and in the fruit and dairy belt of southern Ontario. Fully half of Canada's Class I farmland is in the latter province—precisely the region where acid rain attains some of its greatest peaks of potency.

Mobilized by the media and environmental groups, public opinion in Canada had begun to bring pressure to bear on governments to do something about acid rain by the latter part of the 70s. The pressure prompted official inquiries: one by the Ontario Legislature, which released its findings in 1979, and a second by a special federal Parliamentary Subcommittee on Acid Rain, which revealed its conclusions in 1980–81.

These official reports confirmed many Canadian observers' worst fears, revealing that the actual and potential damages were, if anything, greater than expected. The federal Parliamentary report, titled *Still Waters: The Chilling Reality of Acid Rain*, did not mince words. Wrote its authors: "Canada is facing the greatest environmental threat in the 114 years of our existence as a nation. . . . There was an immediate and firm consensus among all members [of the subcommittee] that the seriousness of the problem and the need for a solution transcended all political affiliations."

Canadians had realized quite early that the sources of danger were located in *both* Canada and the United States, thus posing a dual control problem. They would not only have to curb their own emissions but would also have to persuade their southern neighbors to do likewise.

Unfortunately, the politicians who govern America's staunchest ally and closest international trading partner have been unable to do either. Domestically, there are two major stumbling blocks to Canada's emission control: the federal nature of the country's political structure and the economic and political clout of Canada's major polluters. Unlike the United States, where a civil war and years of legislative evolution have made the old battle cry of "state's rights" a virtual dead letter, Canada's federal structure is alive and well. A Canadian province has considerably more autonomy than an American state, and that autonomy extends to the question of pollution controls. The federal government in Ottawa may set national pollution standards, but it has no mandatory responsibility to enforce them. That job is left to the provinces. In addition, national sulphur dioxide limits, set at 0.3 parts per million in ambient air, do not include any limit on sulphates or acids, such as H_2SO_4, which fall in places distant from the original emission sources.

The history of Canada's domestic efforts at acid rain control is thus a history chiefly of the struggle of the Ontario and Quebec governments to impose their will on the three heaviest emitters in the country, Inco Limited, Ontario Hydro and Noranda Mines Limited, all of whom are major employers and major political forces with which to reckon.

The symbolic importance of Inco's Sudbury Superstack, the single worst source of sulphur pollution in the world, has focussed primary attention on Ontario's efforts to regulate the multinational nickel giant. Indeed, the existence of the Sudbury smelter has provided a handy stick with which American polluters can beat back Canadian attempts to make the United States clean up. "How about cleaning up your own backyard first?" has been the battle cry of many an irate Ohio utility, whose public relations staffs point corporate fingers straight at Sudbury.

The finger-pointers neglect to mention, of course, that Inco's corporate history reveals the company to have been heavily dominated by American interests from 1881 to 1972. Even today, U.S. influence appears at least as strong as Canadian in the running of the firm. For decades the company was controlled by interests associated with those of the empire founded by New York financier J. P. Morgan. A senior partner of the Wall Street law firm of Sullivan and Cromwell has traditionally had a seat on Inco's board of directors. Inco's general counsel was at one time John Foster Dulles, the famed red-baiting secretary of state of the Eisenhower administration.

According to Wallace Clement, in *Continental Corporate Power* (1977 edition): "It is clear that Inco has historically been controlled from the United States by the Morgan interests, although without a U.S. corporation acting as parent. As recently as 1972, twelve of its twenty-four directors were U.S. residents, along with eight Canadian residents, three from Britain and one other. . . . Changes between 1972 and 1975 have led to a board made up of thirteen Canadian residents,

eleven U.S. residents and one other . . . [from among Inco's]
executives, who are mainly U.S. and Canadian. It is the em-
bodiment, in one company, of continental capitalism."

Current Inco chairman Charles F. Baird is a former U.S. un-
dersecretary of the Navy. Other Inco board alumni include
Exxon's J. K. Jamieson and Laurence Rockefeller, grandson of
the founder of Standard Oil. Branding Inco a "Canadian" of-
fender in an effort to duck the United States' responsibility for
the acid rain phenomenon is, obviously, somewhat less than
fair.

Of course, regardless of who wields power in Inco's board-
rooms, it remains the Ontario government's responsibility to
set and enforce environmental regulations capable of curbing
the Superstack's noxious eruptions. Until 1983, however,
when the final stage of a 1980 Ministry of the Environment
pollution control order "with teeth" at long last came into force
against Inco, the record of provincial efforts to reduce the company's emissions had been consistently feeble.

As noted in Chapter One, the government made its first hesitant step toward controlling Inco's wastes in 1970, when the
company was ordered to reduce its SO_2 emissions from 5,200
tons per day to 4,400 tons by the end of 1974, to 3,600 tons
by 1976 and to 750 tons per day by the end of 1978. When
1978 came, however, the company had not complied with the
order and the Ontario government's response was, essentially,
to do nothing. Snapped an angry editorial in the *Toronto Globe
and Mail*:

> We are now halfway through 1978 and Inco is still emitting
> 3,600 tons a day. Far from penalizing the company, however,
> the ministry has issued a new order permitting Inco to maintain
> that level until June 30, 1982, asking only for a report by De-
> cember, 1979 'evaluating the feasibility of controlling' the
> smelter's pollution. . . .
> If the problem of Inco's pollution was considered serious

enough to warrant stiff action in 1970, and if the ministry's own reports belie its contention that damage by the chemical waste in the Sudbury region has 'essentially been resolved,' there is no reason to believe the problem has mysteriously disappeared. If Minister George McCague knows of such a reason—a reason as yet not made public and one which will explain his ministry's incomprehensible actions—he owes it to the Ontario public to share that reason with it.

Not until February 1979, after McCague had been shuffled out of his post, did the real reasons surface. They came out in hearings conducted by the provincial Legislature's Resources and Development Committee, which revealed that Inco and government officials had been meeting regularly since 1970 in private sessions, sessions in which Inco insisted repeatedly that pollution abatement was impossible. As Ross Howard and Michael Perley reported in *Acid Rain*:

> Cost to Inco was the focal point of the private meetings over the years. The company argued it could not afford $300 million for even a partial reduction below 3,600 tons per day. . . .
>
> Inco's experts dismissed scrubbers like those applied to coal plants and smaller smelters elsewhere. Inco said it would cost billions of dollars to rebuild a new and clean smelter. Who could question the experts? . . . There was one other option, Inco suggested. It could cut emissions as required by simply cutting production of nickel. Unfortunately, this would mean closing seven of the ten mines in Sudbury, most of the smelter, a refinery in Port Colborne and other facilities, and dropping at least 6,500 workers. Inco would be forced to abandon Sudbury. . . . It was a warning. When the deadline rolled close, the Ontario government backed off.

Not until 1980, a full decade after the original control order, was anything done to reduce the 3,600-ton-per-day limit. By 1980, the issue of acid rain had assumed major proportions in Canada and the impetus for control was all but impossible for politicians to resist. Another order, this time issued as a non-appealable "Order in Council," was given to Inco, requiring the company to cut emissions by stages to a low of 1,950 tons per day by January 1983. This final emission level was, of course, considerably higher than the original call for a drop to 750 tons per day, and there was no certainty that the company would not attempt to defy it. Because of the depressed world market for nickel, the company's smelter was shut down until mid-1983 and was producing below capacity most of the time since, so that its total emissions would fall below the limit. What might happen in future should production pick up again is anyone's guess.

The Ontario government's efforts to reduce the oxide emissions of Ontario Hydro have been just as desultory, as have the efforts of the Quebec government to reduce Noranda Mines' emissions from its smelter at Rouyn-Noranda, Quebec, and the federal government's effort to tighten its automobile nitrogen oxide emission standards, which are lower than those of the United States.

As already mentioned, Ontario Hydro is a Crown corporation some of whose executives have friendly ties to Premier William Davis. With a massive investment in the construction of nuclear generating stations, Ontario Hydro has obviously been moving away from coal for several years, but its fossil-fuel plants still managed to keep it among the top ten sulphur emitters in the country well into the 1980s. As noted previously, although Hydro technicians had actually been responsible for the early progress in scrubber design, none of the company's coal-burning stations have benefited from that knowledge. Nor are they likely to in the future.

Probably the best example of Hydro's resistance to abatement is its controversial Atikokan generating station in Northwestern Ontario, which sparked an international controversy between Ontario, Minnesota and the U.S. federal government and gave U.S. government and industry spokesmen still another stick with which to beat off Canadian attempts to prompt U.S. abatement action.

Originally approved in 1973 as an 800-megawatt station, the coal-fired plant was to be built—without any form of pollution controls on its 650-foot smokestack—only 12 miles from two of the continent's most beautiful and ecologically fragile wilderness areas: Ontario's Quetico Provincial Park and Minnesota's Boundary Waters Canoe area. The maze of lakes and streams in these parks, considered the finest canoe-camping wilderness in North America, are highly sensitive to acidification, and opponents of the Hydro project on both sides of the border feared the emissions from the Atikokan plant would be just enough to push many of the area's lakes over the edge to acid-death. The Minnesota government, eventually seconded by Washington, objected fiercely to Hydro's plans, filing formal protests and demanding that the plant, if it had to be built, should include scrubbers. Hydro and the Ontario government dismissed all objections, and it was not until 1979 that changes were made in construction plans.

It was in 1979 that Hydro decided to slash the size of the project by 50 percent, not because of any desire to allay pollution, but because highly publicized studies had shown that the utility's endless expansions had created a 40 percent province-wide power surplus, and the extra power of Atikokan was simply not needed. Recalcitrant to the last, however, Hydro insisted that the scaled-down plant would not be equipped with pollution controls, either.

Not until 1981, in the midst of a provincial election compaign in which the government was running scared, did the Ministry of the Environment finally issue a control order against Hydro, demanding that it reduce emissions from 550,000 tons per year in 1981 to 450,000 tons by 1986 and

300,000 tons by 1990, throughout its province-wide generating system. The utility at first bowed, agreeing to make the reductions and announcing that it would install scrubbers.

It did not take long, however, to manifest its bad faith. First, Hydro announced that it was planning to sell its surplus power to the American General Public Utilities (owners of the ill-fated Three Mile Island plant), and that almost all of the power to be sold would be supplied by coal-fired plants with no scrubbers. Thus, emissions would actually be increasing in the short term, until abatement equipment was installed. The GPU deal eventually fell through, but Hydro then compounded the impression of ill will by announcing that, despite its earlier promises, scrubbers would not be installed on its coal plants after all.

Any reductions in emissions were apparently to be accomplished via the expedient of switching over to nuclear power.

Meanwhile, in Quebec, the provincial government has had little success in convincing Noranda Mines to reduce the emissions from its smelters. The company's reaction to such demands has been to threaten a shut-down. In its brief to the federal subcommittee on acid rain, Noranda pointedly warned that closing its smelters would cost Quebec 3,600 to 8,700 jobs. The government in Quebec City has ordered Noranda to reduce its emissions by 40 percent by 1985, but whether it can enforce its order or, like Ontario when faced with Inco's closure threats, it will back down remains to be seen.

Political impotence to force pollution abatement is not limited in Canada to provincial governments. The federal government in Ottawa has also demonstrated a high degree of apathy where domestic policy is concerned. This is most apparent in connection with Ottawa's failure to tighten its vehicle nitrogen oxide emissions standards. Although automotive emissions are responsible for more than half of Canada's NO_x pollution, federally set emission standards continue to allow more than three times as many emissions per vehicle mile as do the standards in the United States. In Canada, the limit is 3.1 grams of NO_x per vehicle mile, compared to 1 gram per mile in the United States.

As the *Toronto Globe and Mail* reported in July 1983, "Adele Hurley [of the Canadian Coalition on Acid Rain] is particularly disturbed that Canada may take as long as four more years to tighten the controls. She said that consultants preparing reports for Environment Canada are going to miss this year's deadline for a study on the problem and traditionally Canada has given car makers three years' lead time to modify pollution control equipment.

"By missing the August deadline for such notification it would delay controls until the 1987 model year, she said."

As a subsequent *Globe and Mail* editorial complained:

> This does more than embarrass, more than undermine our piety. It adds greatly to the practical difficulties of people like Adele Hurley, who lobbies in Washington for clean air laws. Her activities might be more fruitful there if she did not regularly run into the argument that we are not really in a position to preach about clean air when we are so lax about a major source of pollution.

The *Globe's* point was, of course, well taken. All of these domestic pollution control failures, whether on the part of Ontario, Quebec or the federal bureaucracy in Ottawa, have made it infinitely more difficult for Canadian negotiators to make a convincing case in Washington. And this self-induced handicap is tragic, for the truth is that, regardless of how poorly Canada's politicians have performed in controlling their own country's emissions, the people of Canada are receiving three to four times as much acidic pollution from the United States as they themselves send southward. Even if Canada were to curtail all of its own oxide emissions tomorrow, Canadian lakes, forests and people as well would continue to die by their "Good Neighbor's" hand.

American officials, of course, have paid a certain amount of lip service to Canada's predicament. Ironically, it was even the United States, in a May 1978 Senate resolution criticizing Ontario Hydro's Atikokan construction plans, that first raised acid deposition to the status of an international issue. That Senate resolution sparked Canadian federal and provincial statements to the effect that a joint U.S./Canada agreement, similar to the Great Lakes Water Quality Agreement of 1978 regulating water pollution, might be needed to solve the international problem posed by acid rain.

Of course, such statements served an ulterior political purpose. By focussing on the need for international action, Canadian politicians could deflect domestic criticism of their own failure to control local polluters. An "after you, Alphonse" scenario could be established, with Canadians insisting that Americans should "go first." American politicians were quick to see the merits of this approach and replied in kind.

Gradually, however, despite the ambivalent attitude on both sides of the border, what looked like a realistic dialogue began. The waffling politicians found themselves backing into a series of negotiations that took on a life of their own. In Canada the impetus to begin taking such negotiations seriously was provided by the announcement in July 1979 of then-president Jimmy Carter's plans, under his national energy program, to convert more than 50 oil-fired electric power plants in 16 states to coal—with no provision for any environmental safeguards to offset the expected massive increase in sulphur dioxide emissions. The news spelled disaster for Canada, where headlines blared: "Acid Rain Threat Ignored, Carter Sets '85 Coal Goal—Environmental Safeguards Dropped Despite Plea from Ottawa."

Shortly afterward, as if to ease the blow, a "Joint Statement on Transboundary Air Quality" was released by both governments, in which Washington and Ottawa pledged to work toward a future air pollution treaty. This "agreement to agree" was followed in 1980 by a more formal "Memorandum of Intent Concerning Transboundary Air Pollution," which also pledged to work toward a treaty and set up several joint U.S./Canada technical and scientific "work groups" to help prepare for and conduct the formal negotiations. The work groups actually prepared several valuable reports, and Canadians began to take hope that real progress might be made toward offsetting the worst effects of the Carter "go-coal" program.

Then the Reagan administration came to power, and suddenly all bets were off.

Committed to a program of repealing or weakening enforcement of the body of environmental laws and regulations passed during previous administrations, the new President's appointees set about what one observer called "an aggressive pursuit of de-regulation and government withdrawal from pollution control and research." Writes Stephen Clarkson in *Canada and the Reagan Challenge*:

> Attempts made in the seventies to regulate industry's pollution levels had generated much of the business hostility to regulation that had propelled Reagan's Republican team to office. The Environmental Protection Agency fell victim to the new administration's dual thrust to reduce the size of government and restrict the extent of regulation. A drastic change was made in its personnel. As part of the natural replacement of Democrats by Republicans a whole new hierarchy moved in to replace the top three or four levels of officials in the agency. . . .
>
> The guarantee that the EPA would not be able to police the existing regulations could be seen in the agency's budget cut of almost 26 percent from fiscal year 1981 to $961 million in fiscal

year 1983. Within less than two years the headquarters staff
was to fall by 24 percent to 8,465 employees, leading critics to
charge that the Reagan administration was deliberately demol-
ishing the environmental agency.

The EPA, which had been an ally of Canada in Carter's court,
had become an adversary in Reagan's.

The attempt, through John Dingell's committee, to scuttle
the Clean Air Act, the efforts of Secretary of the Interior James
Watt to transfer large tracts of public land and resources to private developers at bargain prices, the struggles of EPA admin-
istrator Ann Gorsuch and her aides as they lurched from scandal to scandal, presented a decidedly discouraging spectacle to
Canadians.

The administration's efforts would eventually end in disaster
for its own appointees, as both Watt and Gorsuch, embroiled
in seemingly constant battles with Congressional committees
and media representatives on the trail of scandals, were finally
forced to resign. Gorsuch lieutenant Rita Lavelle, administra-
tor of the EPA's hazardous waste disposal programs, would end
up jailed for perjury after being convicted of lying to Congress
about her handling of the $1.6 billion Superfund for waste
clean up. Such downfalls, however, brought little comfort to
ordinary Canadians, who could only watch in frustration as the
Reagan term wore on and their environment continued to de-
teriorate under its growing acid burden.

An early casualty in the Reagan assault were the U.S./Can-
ada negotiations aimed at an eventual transboundary air pollution treaty. In the summer of 1981, the U.S. abruptly with-
drew support for one of the key working group projects—that
concerned with assessing alternative emission control scenarios—and began what seemed to Canadians an almost systematic attempt to wreck the talks.

Complained Raymond Robinson, chairman of the Canadian
Environmental Assessment Review Office, "We were treated

to the sight of non-experts rewriting the work group conclusions and unhappy scientists [formally part of the U.S. team]
being quietly reassigned. . . .

"Our scientific experts have attended scheduled meetings
and had virtually no one turn up on the United States' side or
had people arrive whom they had never before seen. Despite
the frustration of operating under such conditions, our people
have occasionally succeeded in laboriously putting together a
draft only to have it greatly changed by United States officials
who had not been involved in the discussions that produced
it."

The situation, he said, was "distressing, even absurd."

In February 1982, the Canadian team offered a possible
treaty formula, submitting it to U.S. negotiators for consideration. The draft called for a 50 percent cutback in emissions of
sulphur dioxide in both Eastern Canada and the United States.
The proposal was formally rejected by the United States in
June, after which Canadian Environment Minister John Rob-
erts publicly questioned the value of continuing negotiations.
Raymond Robinson charged that the United States was risking
the destruction of "over 70 years of respect for principle and
practical cooperation in Canada/United States environmental
relations." By then, many Canadians regarded the United
States as hopelessly stubborn and bargaining in bad faith.

Canadian attempts to alter the direction of U.S. policy had
not been restricted to the diplomatic and scientific talks aimed
at a transboundary treaty. Other avenues had also been ex-
plored. In March 1981, for example, lawyers retained by the
Ontario government filed a brief with the EPA, intervening in
a case involving the relaxation of SO_2 emission limits for 18
coal-burning power stations in Ohio. The province also inter-
vened in support of New York and Pennsylvania in suits filed
by those states against 50 power stations in the Midwest.

Governments have not been alone in the struggle. A citizens group, the Canadian Coalition on Acid Rain referred to in the *Globe and Mail* article quoted previously, was organized in December 1980 to bring together various business, environmental and recreation groups with a common interest in curbing acid deposition. Its membership includes such diverse entities as the Federation of Ontario Cottagers Associations, Resorts Ontario, the Allied Boating Association of Canada, the United Auto Workers of Canada and the Ontario Lung Association. The coalition has hired and financed a full-time lobbyist to present the case for clean air in Washington.

The Canadian National Film Board even produced a documentary film, *Acid Rain: Requiem or Recovery?*, for showing in the United States. The film, produced by the same organization that won the Academy Award in 1983 for *If You Love This Planet*, a documentary on the medical effects of nuclear war, was promptly branded "political propaganda" by the Reagan administration and required to carry a disclaimer noting that it was "registered with the Department of Justice in Washington under the Foreign Agents Registration Act." Finding their motion pictures lumped in the same mound with Communist or Nazi propaganda was a new experience for Canadians. Even though the requirement to register was later ruled unconstitutional by a U.S. federal judge, the insult still rankles.

Given such a background, and the fact that President Reagan's 1984 State of the Union address still promised no firm action on acid rain, the average Canadian voter could be excused if he was pessimistic about escaping sulphur and nitrogen pollution. Neither the half-hearted action of his federal and provincial governments to regulate polluters at home nor the stubborn resistance of the administration in Washington would seem to hold out a hopeful prospect.

Hope, nevertheless, does exist. Its faint glimmerings can be made out, still radiating from the heart of that institution beloved of Jeffersonian democrats because of its nearness to the people—the U.S. Congress.

Says the Canadian Coalition on Acid Rain's Adele Hurley: "What Canadians often don't remember is that Congress passes the laws, not the White House. And the issue is now in Congress. It could go either way. That's our window in time. The bill has to be well along in the process before the presidential campaigns are in full swing, and the vote has to be early, early in 1984, because who's going to want to do Clean Air once we get into the primaries? We only have a few months, otherwise the issue may go away for another three years.

"The scientists are telling us that we've got to hurry now; we're already behind schedule if we want to save the environment. If we wait another few years to get the legislation, plus five more years to install the abatement equipment, we've probably lost all the lake systems. You've lost it. It's finished.

"This is our window. We can't afford to wait."

Eight

Human Dimensions

S tatues dissolving and guns rusting, children choking and soil becoming poisoned, trees withering, rocks blackening.

And the trout float belly-up.

E. F. Schumacher said it well in his classic *Small is Beautiful*: "Modern industry seems to be inefficient to a degree that surpasses one's ordinary powers of imagination. Its inefficiency therefore remains unnoticed."

Because it may not seem profitable, in the narrowest, most immediate sense, for pollution to be abated, it is allowed to go on, destroying the only real "profit" that could be reaped from an entire civilization—the assurance of security, well-being and personal growth for which our species went to the trouble of creating a civilization in the first place.

Man modifies his environment, as a bird builds a nest or a beaver its lodge, in order to find greater security, to increase his chances of survival and to enrich his brief, mysterious passage through life. If, however, our modifications achieve the opposite—tearing away security, threatening survival and impoverishing our lives—we would be a maladapted species indeed to keep on with them. If the rules of natural selection obtain, a species so deluded as to cling to such errors would be doomed to auto-extinction.

Looked at from the outside, through the eyes of objectivity, the toxins with which we are showering ourselves, like ashes tossed into the air to fall back on our own heads, are evidence not of national wealth or power but of foolishness. What other creatures would be so demented as to deliberately foul their own nests, cut off their own food supply, poison their own young, and regard the results as profitable?

Yet there are those who still argue that there is no other way, that the alternatives are "too expensive." Perhaps they are, if the terms of reference by which the alternatives are judged are so rigidly defined as to exclude three quarters of reality. But there is no need to trash ourselves or our children in order to adhere to a mathematical formula in a ledger book. There is no inexorable law of economics that says we *must* wreck the world. In their limited spheres and with imperfect means, companies like Kidd Creek Mines have already proven that. There is another way, and it need not be unprofitable, even in the narrow sense. What is needed is a sense of balance, of good will, and a little ingenuity.

Stopgap measures will be needed in the short run, technological tourniquets to meet the emergencies caused by a faulty energy delivery system and a faulty set of priorities. In this sense, the installation of scrubbers may be necessary and a bill like Waxman and Sikorski's HR-3400 required.

But tourniquets can't be worn forever, or the limbs they are intended to save may rot with gangrene. Sooner or later a genuine cure must take place and the tourniquets be removed.

The spreading gray fields of calcium sulphate that fill the land around the Conesville power station can't keep growing endlessly.

The real problem is that the *system* is wrong, and the philosophy behind it defective. Until these things are changed pressure groups, legislators, engineers and business executives will continually be running from emergency to emergency, from acid rain to toxic wastes to out-of-control capital costs, trying to contain ever-new breakdowns.

Wrote Murray Bookchin, in his perceptive 1975 essay *Energy, Ecotechnocracy and Ecology* (republished in his 1980 book, *Toward an Ecological Society*):

> To make solar energy alone, or wind power alone, or methane alone the exclusive "solution" to our energy problems would be as regressive as adopting nuclear energy. Let us grant that solar energy, for example, may prove to be environmentally far less harmful and more efficient than conventional forms. But to view it as the exclusive source of energy presupposes a mentality and sensibility that leaves untouched the industrial apparatus and the competitive, profit-oriented social relations that threaten the viability of the biosphere.
>
> In all other spheres of life, growth would still be pursued for its own sake, and consumption for its own sake, followed eventually by the simplification of the planet to a point which would resemble a more remote geological age in the evolution of the organic world.
>
> Conceptually, the beauty of "alternate energy" has been not merely its efficiency and its diminution of pollutants, but the ecological interaction of solar collectors, wind generators and methane digesters with each other and with many other sources of energy including wood, water—and yes, coal and petroleum where necessary—to produce a new energy pattern, one that is artistically tailored to the ecosystem in which it is located.

In other words, if an energy system is out of tune with its environment, including the *human* environment, no amount of tinkering with it will make it work. And that very human environment is of crucial importance, because the human species is, after all, part of nature. Whatever is dangerous or unhealthy or unhappy for our own species is very likely going to be so for other species as well.

The human world and the so-called "natural world" are not really separate, isolated from each other and mutually hostile. They are part of the same reality. If the human species is not to spin out of control in nature like multiplying cancer cells in a body, then human systems must not spin out of the control of the individual person they are intended to serve.

In part, it is a question of scale. Bookchin continues:

> Alternate energy, if it is to form the basis for a new ecotechnology, would have to be scaled to human dimensions. Simply put, this means that corporate gigantism with its immense, incomprehensible industrial installations would have to be replaced by small units which people could comprehend and directly manage by themselves. No longer would they require the intervention of industrial bureaucrats, political technocrats, and a species of "environmentalist" who seek merely to engineer "natural resources" to suit the demands of an inherently irrational and anti-ecological society. No longer would people be separated from the means whereby they satisfied their material needs by a suprahuman technology with its attendant "experts" and "managers."
>
> Indeed, following from the attempt to achieve a variegated energy pattern and an ecotechnology scaled to human dimensions, they would be obliged to decentralize their cities as well as their industrial apparatus into new ecocommunities—communities that would be based on direct face-to-face relations and mutual aid.

In the final analysis, the long-term treatment for such symptoms of environmental maladaptation as acid rain is not to be found in the simple application of technical or mechanical band-aids, or in throwing money—whether private capital or taxes siphoned from everyone's pockets—into larger and larger clean-up funds. The polluter never really pays, he just passes the cost along, in higher utility rates or the bigger chunk the IRS carves out of each paycheck.

The real solution lies in treating the disease: the massive, unwieldy, overcomplicated and nonaccountable energy system. In a sense, the system is like a supertanker at sea running at top speed. Because of its bulk, it builds up such momentum that it cannot be stopped or turned in less than a mile. If a nearby obstacle presents itself the helmsman can do nothing but watch the crash.

The exact forms the necessary changes should take are beyond the scope of this book, but some of the general principles on which they might be based are perceptible.

Decentralization is a key element. A town the author of this book has visited obtains its electrical power from the province-wide grid of Ontario Hydro, an immense, unmanageable system whose bureaucracy is so tangled that the provincial legislature cannot control it and whose insatiable growth has required such massive borrowing that the future of Ontario has been literally mortgaged by it. Yet a block from the local beer store is a dam, located at one end of a lake, and sitting by the side of the road are the rusting, ruined pieces of machinery that once formed part of a local generating station. The dam is not used. The water spills over it, dropping down to the stream level below, to no purpose. Rebuilt, re-established and operated by local people, this same dam could power the town and a good part of the surrounding township, cleanly, with no acid rain or nuclear wastes to eliminate. Unfortunately the laws and regulations, the narrow version of what is profitable and what is not profitable, stand in the way. A centralized system, headquartered in a city hundreds of miles away, all but incomprehensible in its scale and expenses, holds sway. Its errors, including nuclear waste spills, reactor breakdowns and tons of sulphur dioxide, may kill us or bankrupt us before its directors admit it is not efficient.

Other key elements are ingenuity, a sense of adventure and a basic faith in the personal responsibility of ordinary people. The kind of ingenuity that remade Dow Chemical's Sarnia plant or Kidd Creek's smelter can be applied in company after company, community after community. The laws of state and province can be refashioned, and the attitudes of boards of directors—that "most important" factor mentioned by Professors Cawsey and Richardson—can encourage it.

Failure to make such changes may not prevent the implementation of short-term "fixes" adequate to curtail, say, sulphur and nitrogen emissions for the next ten years. But it will virtually guarantee the appearance, in short order, of new, equally threatening problems, problems born of the solutions.

Only if a fundamental shift in thinking occurs, a shift that allows us to readjust our priorities and rethink our goals, will an energy system we can control be possible.

Appendix A:
Further Sources

No popular book can hope to cover completely a phenomenon as complex and wide ranging as that of acid deposition. At best, a journalistic approach can only provide an introduction—a sort of survey course—and point readers in the right direction for further research on their own.

Following is a list of publications and groups concerned with the effects of acid deposition. Readers who want more than a surface knowledge of the issue can consult any one of them profitably.

General Background

Howard, Ross and Perley, Michael. *Acid Rain*. New York: Mc-Graw-Hill, 1982.

An excellent general discussion of the acid rain problem, with good political analyses of internal Canadian politics and Canadian/American relations during the Carter years. One of the co-authors is currently employed by the Canadian Coalition on Acid Rain.

Boyle, Robert H. and Boyle, R. Alexander. *Acid Rain*. New York: Schocken Books, 1983.

A reliable, "quick read" introduction to the question with a bit more on U.S. politics than the Howard/Perley book.

Weller, Phil and the Waterloo Public Interest Research Group. *Acid Rain, the Silent Crisis*. Kitchener, Ontario: Between the Lines Press, 1980.

Written in outline style, this short introductory book deals chiefly with Canada.

Subcommittee on Acid Rain, Report of. *Still Waters: The Chilling Reality of Acid Rain.* Ottawa, Ontario: Ministry of Supply and Services, 1981.
The official report of the Canadian Parliamentary Subcommittee on Acid Rain, this publication contains excellent graphics and statistical material and makes an excellent reference source for schools. Unlike most official government reports, it is obviously intended to educate the layman rather than confuse him.

Swedish Ministry of Agriculture Environment '82 Committee, Report of. *Acidification Today and Tomorrow.* Stockholm, Sweden: Ministry of Agriculture, 1982.
Similar to the Canadian Parliamentary report and, like it, featuring good graphics, this publication describes the European situation, with emphasis on Scandinavian nations. Available from Swedish consulates in the United States and Canada.

Wetstone, Gregory S. and Rosencranz, Armin. *Acid Rain in Europe and North America.* Washington, D.C.: Environmental Law Institute, 1983.
A scholarly yet readable discussion of the legal and diplomatic aspects of the problem, with particularly valuable examinations of international law and treaties dealing with acid rain.

Ackerman, Bruce A. and Hassler, William T. *Clean Coal, Dirty Air.* New Haven: Yale University Press, 1981.
An interesting description of the political background of the U.S. Clean Air Act and amendments, with emphasis on the coal industry and United Mine Workers lobbies.

National Clean Air Coalition. *The Clean Air Act: A Briefing Book for Members of Congress.* Washington, D.C.: National Clean Air Coalition, 1983.
This paperback summary discusses all of the aspects of the act including acid rain, putting the latter in context.

Swift, Jamie and the Development Education Center. *The Big Nickel: Inco at Home and Abroad.* Kitchener, Ontario: Between the Lines Press, 1977.

A critical corporate history of the continent's best-known polluter, including its relations with the union movement.

McKay, Paul. *Electric Empire: The Inside Story of Ontario Hydro.* Kitchener, Ontario: Between the Lines Press, 1983.
The growth of the continent's second-largest electric utility into a dangerous, uncontrolled behemoth is chronicled in detail, showing how its management philosophy developed.

Ninth CRS Policy Seminar, Proceedings of. *Acid Rain Controls and the Economics of the Canadian Nonferrous Mineral Industry.* Kingston, Ontario: Centre for Resource Studies, Queen's University, 1982.
A collection of papers discussing in depth the problems of pollution control in mineral smelters. Included is a paper by Kidd Creek Mines president P. R. Clarke.

Clarkson, Stephen. *Canada and the Reagan Challenge.* Toronto: James Lorimer & Company, 1982.
A broad discussion of U.S./Canadian economic and diplomatic relations under Ronald Reagan, with excellent material on the acid rain dispute.

Scientific Background

National Research Council, Committee on Atmospheric Transport and Chemical Transformation in Acid Precipitation. *Acid Deposition: Atmospheric Processes in Eastern North America.* Washington, D.C.: National Academy Press, 1983.
The landmark U.S. National Academy of Sciences study that showed the link between "what goes up and what comes down," ending industry claims that stack emissions cannot be blamed for actual acid deposition at a given site.

U.S. Environmental Protection Agency, Office of Research and Development. *The Acidic Deposition Phenomenon and Its Effects: Critical Assessment Review Papers, Vols. I & II.* Washington, D.C.: EPA, 1983.
A massive, two-volume study of the physical origins and effects of

acid deposition, presenting a scientifically conservative but highly detailed overview. An absolute must for serious researchers.

NRCC Committee on Scientific Criteria for Environmental Quality. *Acidification in the Canadian Aquatic Environment.* Ottawa, Ontario: National Research Council Canada, 1981 (NRCC No. 18475).

A well-organized and readable survey of current scientific knowledge of the subject at the date of publication. This book is part of a series of similar studies on various subjects. Others in the series that contain information related to acid deposition include:

Copper in the Aquatic Environment (NRCC No. 16454)

Sulphur and Its Inorganic Derivatives in the Canadian Environment (NRCC No. 15015)

Effects of Mercury in the Canadian Environment (NRCC No. 16739)

U.S./Canada Work Group, Interim Report of. *Memorandum of Intent on Transboundary Air Pollution, Phase II Interim Working Paper.* U.S./Canada Work Group, 1981.

A report from the official U.S./Canada Work Group assigned to prepare the scientific groundwork for an eventual international air pollution treaty.

Conference on Acid Rain and the Atlantic Salmon, Proceedings of. *Acid Rain and the Atlantic Salmon.* Saint Andrews, New Brunswick: International Atlantic Salmon Foundation, 1981.

A detailed series of reports on the impact of acid rain on the continent's salmon rivers.

Singer, R., Editor. *Effects of Acidic Precipitation on Benthos.* Springfield, Illinois: North American Benthological Society, 1981.

A series of studies of the effects of acidification on life in freshwater lakes and ponds.

The Institute of Ecology. *International Directory of Acid Precipitation Researchers.* Indianapolis, Indiana: The Institute of Ecology, 1980.

The names and addresses and project titles of groups doing independent research.

General Research Corporation. *Inventory of Acid Deposition Research Projects Funded by the Private Sector.* Palo Alto, California: Electric Power Research Institute, 1983.

A listing of projects with more detailed descriptions than the Ecology Institute booklet's.

Acid Precipitation in Ontario Study. *Acid Sensitivity Survey of Lakes in Ontario.* Toronto: Ontario Ministry of the Environment, 1982.
The pH, alkalinity and other measurements of the major Ontario lakes where acidic deposition takes place.

Wetzel, Robert G. *Limnology.* New York: Saunders College Publishing, 1983.
An introductory text for university-level students in the subject of limnology—the study of freshwater lakes and ponds. It contains basic material essential to understanding the full effects of acid deposition on aquatic environments.

Stocker, H. Stephen and Seager, Spencer L. *Environmental Chemistry: Air and Water Pollution.* Glenview, Illinois: Scott, Foresman and Company, 1976.
An introduction to the chemistry of pollution aimed at a nontechnical audience.

Better Ways

Schumacher, E. F. *Small is Beautiful.* London, England: Sphere Books Limited, 1974.
An international classic; its subtitle, "A Study of Economics as if People Mattered," is self-explanatory.

Bookchin, Murray. *Toward an Ecological Society.* Montreal: Black Rose Books, 1980.
An introduction to the thinking of a remarkable social critic, whose essays collected in this volume include his "Energy, Ecotechnology and Ecology."

Lovins, Amory B. *Soft Energy Paths.* Scranton, Pennsylvania: Harper and Row, 1979.
A pioneering study of alternative energy scenarios whose penetrating analyses of conventional as well as "utopian" systems prove utopia is in the eye of the beholder.

Key Individuals and Groups

Representative Gerry Sikorski (D-Minn.), 414 Cannon House Office Building, Washington, D.C. 20515.

Representative Henry Waxman (D-Calif.) 2415 Rayburn House Office Building, Washington, D.C. 20515.

Senator Robert Stafford (R-Vermont), 4204 Dirksen Senate Office Building, Washington, D.C. 20510.

The National Clean Air Coalition, 530 Seventh Street SE, Washington, D.C. 20003.

The Canadian Coalition on Acid Rain, 112 Saint Clair Avenue West, Suite 504, Toronto, Ontario, Canada M4V 2Y3.

Environmental Protection Agency, Office of Public Awareness, 401 M Street SW, Washington, D.C. 20460.

Pollution Probe, 43 Queen's Park Crescent, University of Toronto, Toronto, Ontario M5S 2C3.

Appendix B:
The Worst Polluters

The total tonnage of sulphur and nitrogen oxides emitted by various smelters and power plants can vary widely from month to month and year to year, depending on the vicissitudes of markets and demand. A decrease in world nickel or copper prices, a series of layoffs or a major strike may slow production at a smelter and cause a drop in emissions. An economic recession, with its attendant slide in industrial demand for electricity, can cause a similar cut in power plant emissions. The Tennessee Valley Authority, until recently one of the worst air-foulers on this continent, has embarked on a clean-up program that is sharply curtailing its pollutant output.

A list of Worst Polluters can thus serve only as a rough indicator of trouble spots, rather than an exact ranking, and may be outdated even before it appears in print. For those who are interested, however, the following lists of sulphur dioxide emitters provide a partial record:

North America's Top Five Coal-Fired Power Plants in Total SO$_2$ Emissions

Plant	1979 Owner	State
1. Paradise	Tennessee Valley Authority	Kentucky
2. Muskingum	American Electric Power Co.	Ohio
3. Gavin	American Electric Power Co.	Ohio
4. Cumberland	Tennessee Valley Authority	Tennessee
5. Monroe	Detroit Edison	Michigan
	1980	
1. Gavin	American Electric Power Co.	Ohio
2. Cumberland	Tennessee Valley Authority	Tennessee
3. Paradise	Tennessee Valley Authority	Kentucky
4. Gibson	Indiana Public Service Commission	Indiana
5. Clifty Creek	American Electric Power Co.	Indiana
	1981	
1. Paradise	Tennessee Valley Authority	Kentucky
2. Cumberland	Tennessee Valley Authority	Tennessee
3. Clifty Creek	American Electric Power Co.	Indiana
4. Monroe	Detroit Edison	Michigan
5. Baldwin	Illinois Power Corp.	Illinois

SOURCE: U.S. EPA and Environment Canada

North America's Top Ten Sources of SO$_2$ Emissions, 1980

Company, Plant	Location	Kilotonnes/year
1. Inco	Ontario	807.5
2. Noranda Mines	Quebec	537.5
3. TVA, Paradise	Kentucky	418.8
4. Inco	Manitoba	333.5
5. AEP, Muskingum	Ohio	306.7
6. AEP, Gavin	Ohio	297.5
7. TVA, Cumberland	Tennessee	296.2
8. AEP, Clifty Creek	Indiana	295.3
9. Illinois Power Corp., Baldwin	Illinois	237.2
10. Detroit Edison, Monroe	Michigan	224.3

SOURCE: U.S. EPA and Environment Canada

Index